W9-BON-192

Basic Computing

with Windows XP

Learning Made Simple

P.K. McBride

AMSTERDAM • BOSTON • HEIDELBERG • LONDON • NEW YORK • OXFORD
PARIS • SAN DIEGO • SAN FRANCISCO • SINGAPORE • SYDNEY • TOKYO

Butterworth-Heinemann is an imprint of Elsevier

Tulare County Library

Butterworth-Heinemann is an imprint of Elsevier
Linacre House, Jordan Hill, Oxford OX2 8DP, UK
30 Corporate Drive, Suite 400, Burlington, MA 01803, USA

First edition 2006

Copyright © 2006 Elsevier Ltd. All rights reserved

No part of this publication may be reproduced, stored in a retrieval
system or transmitted in any form or by any means electronic,
mechanical, photocopying, recording or otherwise without the prior
written permission of the publisher

Permissions may be sought directly from Elsevier's Science &
Technology Rights Department in Oxford, UK: phone (+44) (0) 1865
843830; fax (+44) (0) 1865 853333; email: permissions@elsevier.com.
Alternatively you can submit your request online by visiting the
Elsevier web site at http://elsevier.com/locate/permissions, and
selecting *Obtaining permission to use Elsevier material*

Notice
No responsibility is assumed by the publisher for any injury and/or
damage to persons or property as a matter of products liability,
negligence or otherwise, or from any use or operation of any methods,
products, instructions or ideas contained in the material herein.

TRADEMARKS/REGISTERED TRADEMARKS
Computer hardware and software brand names mentioned in this book
are protected by their respective trademarks and are acknowledged

British Library Cataloguing in Publication Data
A catalogue record for this book is available from the British Library

ISBN-13: 978 0 7506 8184 1
ISBN-10: 0 7506 8184 5

Typeset by P.K. McBride

Icons designed by Sarah Ward © 1994

Printed and bound in Italy

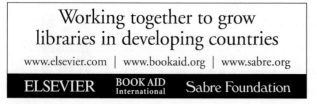

Working together to grow
libraries in developing countries

www.elsevier.com | www.bookaid.org | www.sabre.org

ELSEVIER   BOOK AID
            International   Sabre Foundation

Contents

Preface

The books in the Learning Made Simple series aim to do exactly what it says on the cover – make learning simple.

A Learning Made Simple book:

◆ Is **fully illustrated**: with clearly labelled screenshots.

◆ Is **easy to read**: with brief explanations, and clear instructions.

◆ Is **task-based**: each short section concentrates on one job at a time.

◆ **Builds knowledge**: ideas and techniques are presented in the right order so that your understanding builds progressively as you work through the book.

◆ Is **flexible**: as each section is self-contained, if you know it, you can skip it.

The books in the Learning Made Simple books series are designed with learning in mind, and so do not directly follow the structure of any specific syllabus – but they do cover the content. This book covers Module 2 of the ECDL syllabus and the File Management aspects of New CLAIT. For details of how the sections map against your syllabus, please go to the web site:

http://www.madesimple.co.uk

1 Windows basics

The PC

A desktop PC system typically has these components:

◆ **Monitor** or VDU (Visual Display Unit). On older desktop PCs this is a bulky, cathode ray tube system; modern ones have flat LCD screens. The resolution of a screen is measured in pixels – dots of light. A 17-inch screen, for example, could have a resolutions of up to 1600×1200.

◆ **System unit** – the box containing the 'works'. This may act as a base for the monitor, or stand beside it or on the floor beneath. On the front you should see the front panels of a floppy disk drive and a CD-ROM drive, and two buttons – one is the on/off, the other the reset button. At the back you will find a number of sockets and connections, most with cables plugged into them.

◆ **Keyboard** – though mainly for entering text and numbers, the keys can also be used for controlling the cursor and selecting from menus.

◆ **Mouse** – used for controlling the cursor, allowing you to select items, start programs, draw pictures, and more.

Take note

A desktop PC will normally have attached to it speakers and a printer, and possibly a scanner.

System unit

Monitor

Speaker

Speaker

Keyboard

Mouse

Measuring memory

1 bit = the smallest unit of memory can store either 1 or 0, on or off.

1 byte = 8 bits, can store a number in the range 0 to 255 or a single character of plain text.

1 Kilobyte (Kb) = 1024 bytes, enough for about 150 words of plain text or a simple picture 32 × 32 pixels, like this ☺.

1 Megabyte (Mb) = 1024 Kb, enough for around 300 pages of plain text or 200 pages of formatted text, or a full colour photo 2,000 pixels square.

1 Gigabyte (Gb) = 1024 Mb will hold several hundred very high resolution pictures or a full length video – or countless quantities of text!

RAM (Random Access Memory) = the chips where the PC holds data and program code while it is working.

How can you make a PC go faster?

◆ **Microprocessor power** – and that depends upon the speed of and the amount of integral memory. Currently the most powerful PC chips run at around 3.5 GHz, and have 2 Mb of memory within the chip. (For comparison, the first PC processors ran at 6 MHz and had 64 bytes of integral memory!!) Data often has to be stored somewhere while it is being processed; if it can be stored in the chip, it can be accessed faster.

◆ **Amount of RAM** – currently a bottom of the range home PC will have 256 Mb of RAM; a high-end business PC may have 4 Gb or more. If several applications are running or very large files are being processed, data which is not needed immediately will be stored on the hard drive, then loaded back into RAM when needed, while other data is stored out of the way on the drive. Large amounts of RAM reduce this time-consuming swapping between RAM and drive.

◆ **Number of active applications** – we may only be able to work on one thing at a time, but applications can be active without our direct attention. Some processes, once started, can carry on 'in the background', e.g. printing large files, downloading from the Internet, or sending and receiving e-mail. This all takes processor time, and space in RAM.

Take note

The microprocessor is also known as the **CPU** (Central Processing Unit). It is the chip at the heart of the computer, where instructions are processed and calculations performed.

Processor speed is measured in **Hertz** – cycles per second, and one number is moved or processed each cycle. 3.5 GigaHertz is 3.5 billion cycles per second.

Software

Software can be divided into two major types: operating systems and applications.

Operating systems

An operating system controls the hardware at the lowest level. It tells the computer how to store data in memory, how to read and write to the disks, how to display things on screen, how to get information from the mouse and the keyboard, and so on. It also gives users tools to manage files, and peripherals such as printers and scanners. Finally, an operating system provides a common platform for applications, smoothing over the differences between different types of hardware. When a word-processor wants to read data from a disk, it doesn't need to know what sort of disk it is or how the data is stored – it just asks the operating system to get the file.

◆ **Windows** – in its many versions – is the most widely used operating system today. Developed by Microsoft, and the mainstay of their success, it first appeared in the early 1990s and is now used on around 90% of all desktop PCs. This book is based on Windows XP, the current version at the time of writing.

◆ **Linux**, developed by professional and amateur enthusiasts, is distributed freely (or not-for-profit). It is more efficient and more reliable than Windows, and is the most popular choice for those computers that provide services to the Internet. Linux is for enthusiasts – you normally have to install it yourself and there are few applications that will run on it.

◆ **Mac OS** is Apple's operating system. This is also more efficient and reliable than Windows, but will only work on Apple computers that typically cost 50% or more than the equivalent PC.

Take note

PC stands for 'personal computer' and can refer to any desktop or laptop computer for individual use. However, nowadays it is normally taken to mean a computer compatible with the IBM PC design, running Windows. If it's any other sort, it will be specified, e.g. Apple PC, Linux PC.

Applications

Applications are what make computers useful. They range from heavy-duty business software and data processing, through to the most trivial of games, and tiny utility programs. The most common types of business software are:

Take note

Applications are designed to work with specific operating system. They will usually also work with later versions of the same system, but only because the system is built to handle older software. You can run a Windows 98 program on a Windows XP machine, but not on an Apple.

- ◆ **Word-processing**, used for creating and editing text-based documents, from simple memos to full-colour illustrated reports, brochures – and even books. The most widely-used word processor is Microsoft Word.

- ◆ **Spreadsheets**, such as Microsoft Excel, are used for storing numbers and performing – sometimes very complex – series of calculations on them. They are used in business mainly for recording accounts, budgeting, and forecasting.

- ◆ **Database management systems**, e.g. Microsoft Access, store data and can be used to draw information from it. Common applications include stock control, staff and client/patient/student records.

- ◆ **Presentation software**, such as Microsoft PowerPoint, is used to create slide shows – text and images displayed one page at a time, usually to illustrate talks.

- ◆ **Graphics packages**, e.g. Adobe Illustrator, can create images from scratch, or manipulate images taken from cameras or scanners.

- ◆ **Browsers**, e.g. Internet Explorer, and email systems such as Outlook Express, are essential tools for accessing the World Wide Web and communicating across the Internet.

The Desktop

Windows is a Graphical User Interface (or GUI, pronounced *gooey*). What this means is that you work mainly by using the mouse to point at and click on symbols on the screen, rather than by typing commands. It is largely intuitive – i.e. the obvious thing to do is probably the right thing – and it is tolerant of mistakes. Many can be corrected as long as you tackle them straight away, and many others can be corrected easily, even after time has passed.

One of the key ideas behind the design of Windows is that you should treat the screen as you would a desk, which is why Windows refers to the screen as the *Desktop*. This is where you lay out your papers, books and tools, and you can arrange them to suit your own way of working. You may want to have more than one set of papers on the Desktop at a time – so Windows lets you run several programs at once. You may want to have all your papers visible, for comparing or transferring data; you may want to concentrate on one, but have the others to hand. These – and other arrangements – are all possible.

Each program runs in its own window, and these can be arranged side by side, overlapping, or with the one you are working on filling the Desktop and the others tucked out of the way, but still instantly accessible.

Just as there are many ways of arranging your Desktop, so there are many ways of working with it – in fact, you are sometimes spoilt for choice!

It's your Desktop. How you arrange it, and how you use it is up to you.

◆ What you see on screen when you start Windows depends upon your Desktop settings and the shortcuts – the icons that you can click on to start progams – you are using.

◆ What the screen looks like once you are into your working session, is infinitely variable.

◆ Certain principles always apply and certain things are always there. It is the fact that all Windows applications share a common approach that makes Windows so easy to use.

Shortcuts – instant access to programs, files or folders. You can create shortcuts (**page 69**).

Desktop – you can change the background picture or pattern and its colours (**page 87**).

Menu bar – gives access to a program's commands.

Program windows – adjust their size and placing to suit yourself.

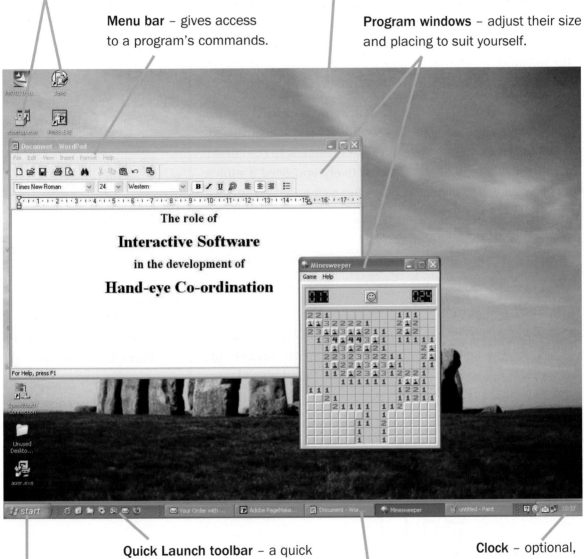

Quick Launch toolbar – a quick way to start key programs.

Clock – optional, but handy.

Start button – you should be able to start any program on your PC from its menu.

Taskbar – when a program is running, it has a button here. Click on a button to open its window and bring it to the front of the Desktop.

7

Taming the mouse

You can't do much in Windows until you have tamed the mouse. It is used for locating the cursor, for selecting from menus, highlighting, moving and changing the size of objects, and much more. It won't bite, but it will wriggle until you have shown it who's in charge.

The mouse and the cursor

There are two main types of mice. One type has a ball beneath. Moving the mouse rolls the ball inside it. The ball turns the sensor rollers and these transmit the movement to the cursor. To control this type of mouse effectively you need a mouse mat or a thin pad of paper - it won't run well on a hard surface.

The other type uses infrared to scan the area beneath and work out which way the mouse has moved. This type needs some kind of image or pattern beneath it - it won't know where it is on a plain surface.

With either type:

♦   If you are so close to the edge of the mat that you cannot move the cursor any further, pick up the mouse and plonk it back into the middle. If the ball doesn't move, the cursor doesn't move.

♦   You can set up the mouse so that when the mouse is moved faster, the cursor moves further. Watch out for this when working on other people's machines.

Mouse actions

Point – move the cursor with your fingers **off** the buttons.

Click the left button to select a file, menu item or other object.

Right-click (click the right button) to open a menu of commands that can be applied to the object beneath the pointer.

Double-click to run programs. You can set the gap between clicks to suit yourself.

Drag – keep the left button down while moving the mouse. Used for resizing, drawing and similar jobs.

Drag and drop – drag an object and release the left button when it is in the right place. Used for moving objects.

Take note

The mouse can be adjusted through the Mouse options in the Control Panel – (see Chapter 6).

Tip

A ball mouse works best if it is clean. If it starts to play up, take out the ball and clean it and the rollers with a damp tissue. Remove any fluff build-up on the roller axles with tweezers.

Key guide

[Esc] – to Escape from trouble. Use it to cancel bad choices.

[Tab] – move between objects on screen.

[Caps Lock] – only put this on when you want to type a lot of capitals. The **Caps Lock** light shows if it is on.

[Shift] – use it for capitals and the symbols on the number keys.

[Ctrl] or [Control] – used with other keys to give keystroke alternatives to mouse commands.

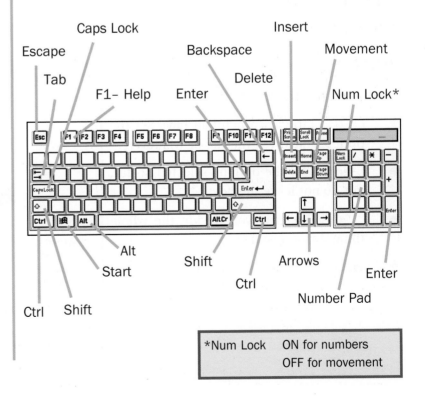 – the same as clicking 🇯 start on the screen.

[Alt] – used, like [Ctrl], with other keys.

[Backspace] – rubs out the character to the left of the text cursor.

[Enter] – used at the end of a piece of text or to start an operation.

[Delete] – deletes files, folders and screen objects. Use with care.

Most Windows XP operations can be handled quite happily by the mouse alone, leaving the keyboard for data entry. However, keys are necessary for some jobs, and if you prefer typing to mousing, it is possible to do most jobs from the keyboard. The relevant ones are shown here.

The function keys

Some operations can be run from these – for instance, **[F1]** starts up the Help system in any Windows application.

The control sets

The **Arrow** keys can often be used instead of the mouse for moving the cursor. Above them are more movement keys, which will let you jump around in text. **[Insert]** and **[Delete]** are also here.

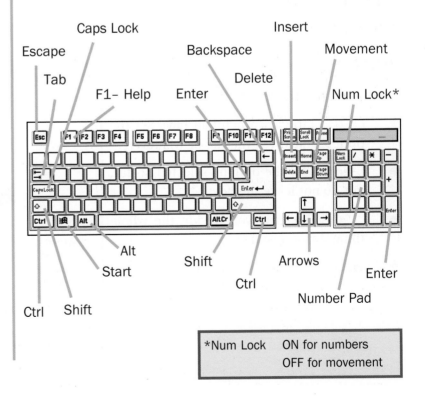

*Num Lock   ON for numbers
           OFF for movement

Making choices

There are many situations where you have to specify a filename or an option. Sometimes you have to type in what you want, but in most cases, it only takes a click of the mouse or a couple of keystrokes.

Menus

To pull one down from the menu bar click on it or press **[Alt]** (the key marked 'Alt') and the underlined letter – usually the initial.

To select an item from a menu, click on it or type its underlined letter.

Some items are *toggles*. Selecting them turns an option on or off – it it is on you will see ✓ beside the name.

▶ after an item shows that another menu leads from it.

If you select an item with three dots ... after it, a dialog box will open to get more information from you.

Dialog boxes

These vary, but will usually have:

◆   OK   to click when you have set the options, selected the file or whatever;

◆   Apply   fix the options selected so far, but do not leave the box;

◆   Cancel   in case you decide the whole thing was a mistake;

◆   ?   to get Help on items in the box.

Click or press **[Alt] + [V]**

Point to open sub-menu

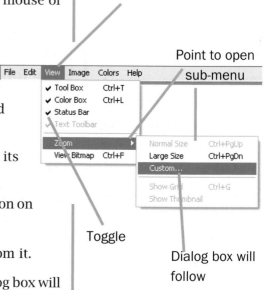

Toggle

Dialog box will follow

Click to get to its panel

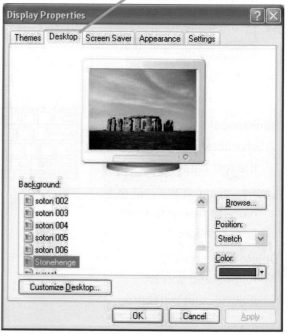

10

Tabs and panels

Some dialog boxes have several sets of options in them, each on a separate panel. These are identified by tabs at the top. Click on a tab to bring its panel to the front. Usually clicking [OK] on any panel will close the whole box. Use [Apply] when you have finished with one panel but want to explore others before closing.

Check boxes

These are used where there are several options, and you can use as many as you like at the same time.

▤ in the box shows that the option has been selected.

If the box is grey and the caption faint, the option is 'greyed out' – not available at that time for the selected item.

Radio buttons

These are used for either/or options. Only one of the set can be selected.

The selected option is shown by black blob in the middle.

Drop-down lists

If a slot has a down arrow button on its right, click the button to drop down a list.

Click on an item in the list to select.

Sliders

Drag the pointer across the slider to adjust the value in one direction or the other.

Most menus drop down from the top bar. The Start menu (page 13) is different – it pops up.

Take note

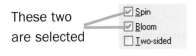

These two are selected

This one please

Take note

Some commands have keyboard shortcuts – often [Ctrl] + a letter. Look out for these on the menus.

Click here...

... to select from the list

Drag on this

Context menus

If you click the right button on almost any object on screen in Windows XP, a short menu will open beside it. This contains a set of commands and options that can be applied to the object.

What is on the menu depends upon the type of object and its *context* – hence the name. Two are shown here to give an idea of the possibilities.

Properties

Most menus have a **Properties** item. The contents of its dialog box also vary according to the nature of the object. For shortcuts, like the one for Jaws PDF Editor shown below, there is a *Shortcut* panel that controls the link to the program. The (hidden) *General* panel has a description of the file – this panel is in every file's Properties box.

Files can be opened, sent to a removable disk or off in the mail, and deleted – amongst other things.

The **Clock** can be adjusted, and as it is on the Taskbar, you can also arrange the screen display from this menu.

Some properties are there for information only ...

... others can be changed

The Start menu

Take note

Windows uses 'document' to mean any file created by any application. A word-processed report is obviously a document, but so is a picture file from a graphics package, data files from spreadsheets, video clips, sound files — any file produced by any program.

Clicking on [☰ start] at the bottom left of the screen opens the Start menu.

At the top left are links to your **browser** and **e-mail** software (normally Internet Explorer and Outlook Express).

Beneath these are links to your **most-used programs** - initially this will be empty. Windows keeps track of which programs you use, and after a few sessions, adds those used most often to the list. You can set how many to include, or remove ones that you no longer use.

At the bottom left is the **All Programs** link (page 14).

At the top right are links to **My Documents** and other folders where documents are commonly stored.

My Recent Documents holds a list of your latest documents. Selecting one from this list will run the relevant application and open the file for you to work on (page 14).

You can configure your PC through the **Control Panel (Chapter 6)**.

Help and Support starts the Help system (page 18).

Use **Search** to track down files on your computer, or to find Web pages or people on the Internet.

Log off... allows the current user to stop using the PC - and for a new user to start - without turning it off.

Turn Off Computer is the only safe way to shut down the PC.

My Start menu – yours will be different as the menu automatically adapts to your usage and can also be customised by you – see **Chapter 6**.

Running a program

The programs already on your PC, and virtually all of those that you install later, will have an entry in the **All Programs** menu. Selecting one from here will run the program, ready for you to start work.

A program can also be run by selecting a document that was created by it. Links to the documents used most recently are stored in the **My Recent Documents** folder.

Basic steps

- **Running a program**

1 Click **start**.

2 Point to **All Programs**.

3 Point to the menu that contains the program – you may have to point to the next menu level.

4 Click on the name to run the program.

- **From documents**

5 Click **start**.

6 Point to **My Recent Documents**.

7 Click on the file to get started on it.

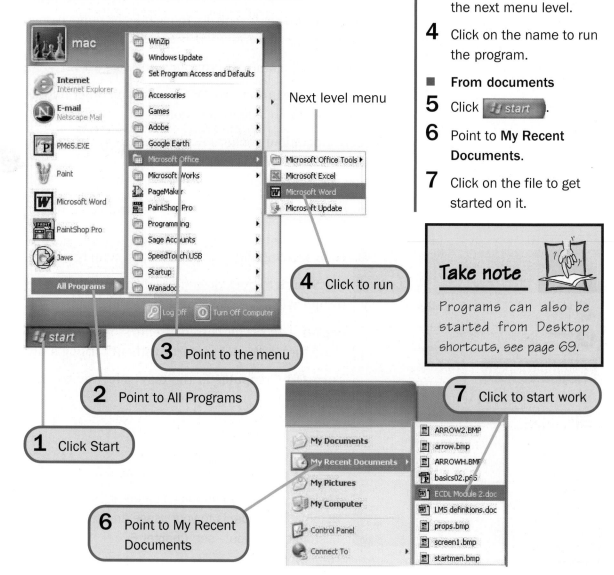

Next level menu

4 Click to run

3 Point to the menu

2 Point to All Programs

1 Click Start

6 Point to My Recent Documents

7 Click to start work

Take note

Programs can also be started from Desktop shortcuts, see page 69.

Basic steps

- **Logging off**

1 Click ⊞ start .

2 Click **Log Off**.

3 If you want to leave your programs active, to return to later, select **Switch User**.

4 If you have finished work, select **Log Off**.

- **Logging on**

5 Switch on the PC.

6 Click on your user name.

7 If you have been given a password, type it in.

Logging off and on

Windows XP is designed to be a multi-user system. It can be used for networks, or can allow several users to share one PC safely. Users must 'log on' at the start of a session, to gain access to their folders and settings. When they have finished they should either turn off the PC (**page 12**) or 'log off', to protect their area from damage – accidental or otherwise – by other users.

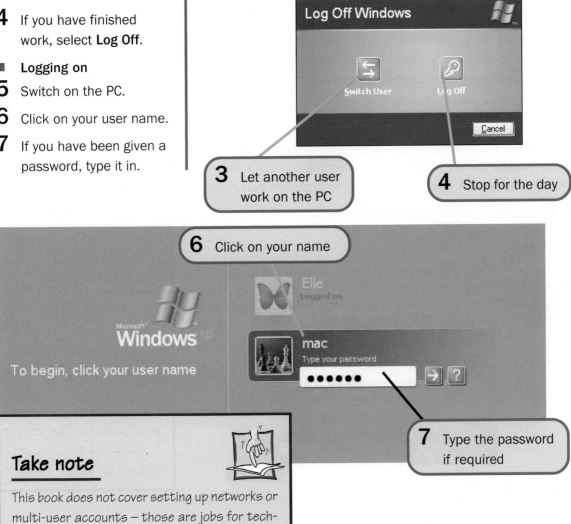

3 Let another user work on the PC

4 Stop for the day

6 Click on your name

7 Type the password if required

Take note

This book does not cover setting up networks or multi-user accounts – those are jobs for technicians at work, and enthusiasts at home.

15

Shutting down

When you have finished work on your computer, you must shut it down properly, and not just turn it off. This is essential. During a working session, application programs and Windows XP itself may have created temporary files – and any data files that you have been editing may still be open in memory and not yet written safely to disk. A proper shutdown closes and stores open files and removes unwanted ones.

Restart

The Turn off computer dialog box offers a **Restart** option. You may need this after installing new software or hardware. It is also one way to solve problems – see opposite for more on this.

There will probably also be a **Stand By** or **Hibernate** option. This will turn off the main power-using parts of your system – the hard drive, monitor and fans – but leave the RAM memory active, and files and programs open, keeping track of what you were doing, so that you can start up quickly when you return.

Systems differ – check your PC's handbook to find out about its Stand By facilities.

Basic steps

1 Click .

2 Select **Turn Off Computer.**

3 Click **Stand By** if you want to get back to work quickly later in the day.

4 Click **Turn Off** if you have finished work completely.

5 Click **Restart** if you need to reset the PC after installing new software.

3 Stand By?

5 Restart

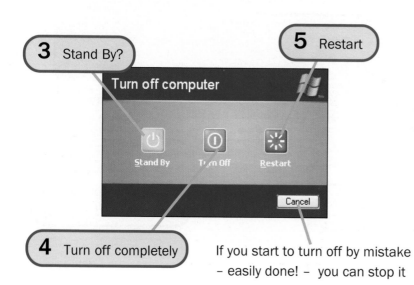

Turn off computer

Stand By   Turn Off   Restart

Cancel

4 Turn off completely

If you start to turn off by mistake – easily done! – you can stop it

Take note

If you simply turn off the PC, or have to use the Restart button, when it starts up again, Windows will offer to check your hard drive(s) in case there is a problem. The check takes a few minutes but is normally worth doing.

Coping with crashes

- **Misbehaving program**

1 Open the program's **File** menu and select **Exit** (or **Close**) – saving files if prompted.

2 Restart the program.

- **Hung system**

3 Press [**Control**] + [**Alt**] + [**Delete**] together.

4 At the **Task Manager** dialog box, select the one marked 'Not Responding' and click [End Task].

5 At the prompt, confirm that you want to end it.

6 Restart the program.

- **Dead keyboard**

7 Press the **Restart** button on front of the PC.

Windows XP is a pretty stable system, but things do go wrong. A 'crash' can can be at several levels.

◆ A program may simply misbehave - it will still run, but not respond or update the screen correctly. Close it – saving any open files - and run it again. If it still behaves badly, close down all your programs and restart the PC.

◆ The system will 'hang' - i.e. nothing is happening and it will not respond to the mouse or normal keyboard commands. If the [**Control**] + [**Alt**] + [**Del**] keystroke works, you can reach the Task Manager to close the offending application, which may get things moving again.

◆ You get a total lock up where it will not pick up [**Control**] + [**Alt**] + [**Del**]. Press the little restart button on the front of the PC. It is there for just these times!

4 End the hung program

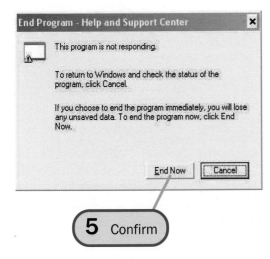

5 Confirm

Help and Support

Windows XP has its own special Help and Support system. It's very comprehensive and has some excellent features, but – most unhelpfully – it looks and feels different from the standard application Help systems. Much the same range of facilities are there, but with new names.

The Home page is the equivalent to Contents. Start to browse through the Help pages from here. It will normally take you four clicks to get from a main topic heading on the Home page, through to a specific page on a Help topic.

1 Click **start** and select **Help and Support Centre**.

Or

2 In My Computer or Windows Explorer, use **Help > Help and Support Center**.

3 Pick a topic from the list on the left.

4 At the next level, click + by a heading to open a list of topics.

Help
Help and Support Center
Is this copy of Windows legal?
About Windows

2 Use Help > Help and Support Center

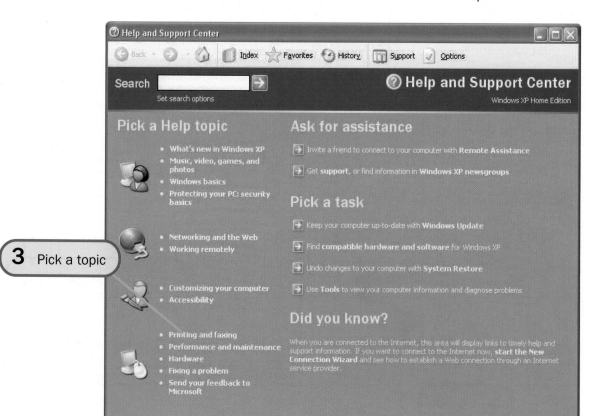

3 Pick a topic

5 Click a sub-topic to display a list of Help pages.

6 Click on a **Fix a problem** or **Pick a task** link to open its page.

5 Pick a sub-topic

Click to return to the Home page

4 Open a heading

6 Click a page link

Some Help links lead to **trouble-shooters**. These will take you through a series of questions and actions to (often) locate and solve the problem

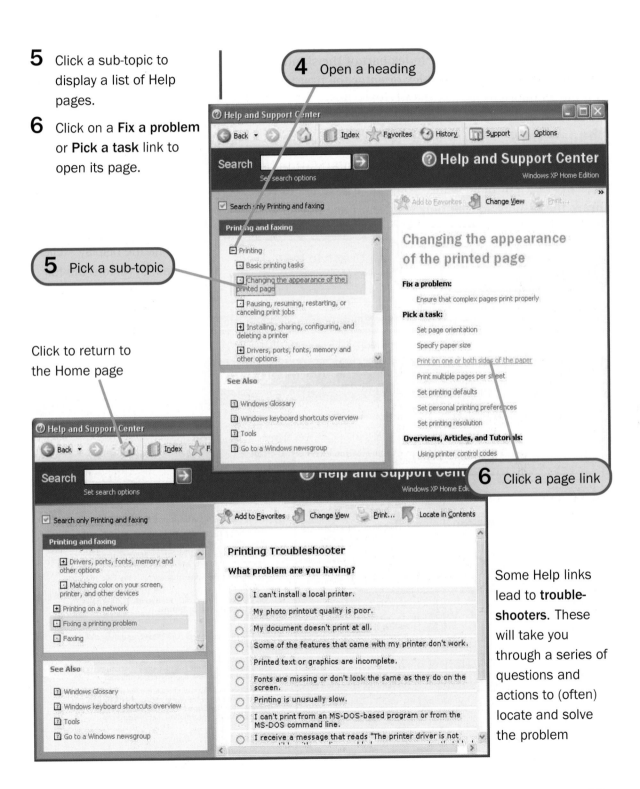

Help Index

This is almost identical to the Index part of the standard Help systems. Scroll through the index or enter the first few letters to jump to the right part of the list.

Change view

In any part of the Help system, once you have opened a Help page in the right-hand pane, you can use Change View to shrink the display so that only the Help page is visible.

Basic steps

1 Switch to the **Index**.

2 Start to type a word, then scroll to the topic.

3 Select an Index entry.

4 Click [Display] – you may have a choice of several Help pages.

5 Click **Change View** to shrink the display – click again to restore the full view if needed.

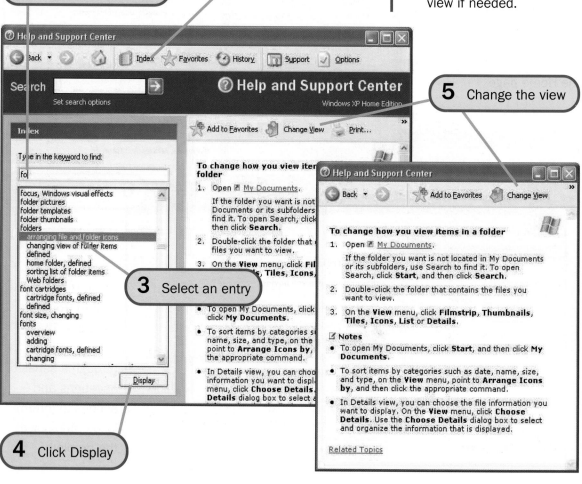

2 Start to type a word

1 Switch to the Index

5 Change the view

3 Select an entry

4 Click Display

Searching for Help

The **Search** box is present on every page of the Help system. The results are grouped in three sets – click the headers to see their results:

◆ **Suggested Topics** are normally the most useful. These are the pages that have been indexed by the keyword;

◆ **Full-text Search Matches** are pages which contain your keywords, but these may only be passing references;

◆ **Microsoft Knowledge Base** draws help from Microsoft's web site and is, of course, only available if you are online.

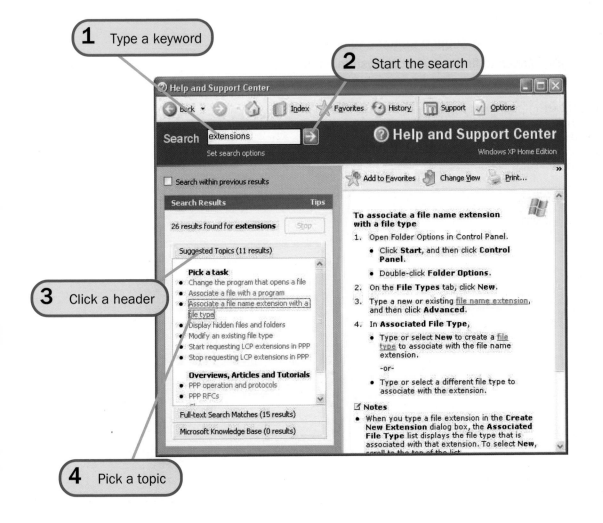

Exercises

1 Start up and log on to your PC, if necessary.

2 Open the Start menu and explore the Programs menu and its submenu. What programs are present on your PC? Which names do you recognise?

3 Go to the Games submenu of the Programs menu, and start any game (except the Internet ones, if they are present). By trial and error, work out how to play the game. This exercise has two serious aims: it should improve your mouse-handling skills, and demonstrate that experimenting with new software can be a good way to learn how to use it.

4 Go to the Help and Support Center and use the Index or Search modes to find out what is 'system information'. Display the system information for your PC.

5 Log off and close down your PC safely.

2 Window control

The window frame

This is more than just a pretty border. It contains all the controls you need for adjusting the display.

Frame edge

This has a control system built into it. When a window is in Restore mode – i.e. smaller than full-screen – you can drag on the edge to make it larger or smaller (see *Changing the size*, **page 31**).

Title bar

This is to remind you of where you are – the title bar of the active application (the one you are using) is blue; the bars of other open applications are grey. The bar is also used for moving the window. Drag on this and the window moves (see *Moving windows*, **page 30**).

Maximize, Minimize and Restore

These buttons change the display mode. Only one of Maximize and Restore will be visible at any one time (see *Window modes*, **page 26**).

Close

One of several ways to close a window and the program that was running in it (see *Closing windows*, **page 33**).

Control menu icon

There is no set image for this icon, as every application has its own, but clicking on whatever is here will open the Control menu. This can be used for changing the screen mode or closing the window (see *Window modes*, **page 26**). Double-clicking this icon will close down the window.

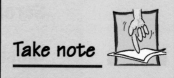

Take note

Most applications can handle several documents at once, each in its own window. These are used in almost the same way as program windows. The applications usually have a **Window** menu containing controls for the document windows.

Take note

The shape of the pointer varies according to the job you are doing at the time, but it changes to the single arrow — ready for a move — when on the Title bar, and to a double-headed arrow — for size adjustment — at an edge.

There are several sets of pointers — the ones used here are the Standard set.

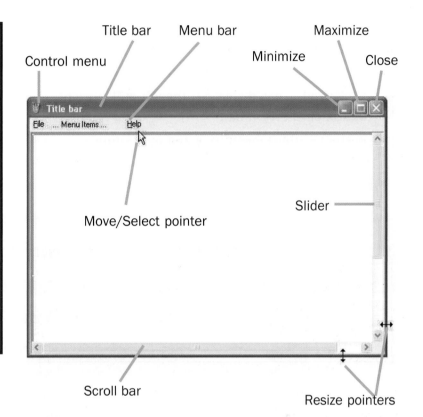

Control menu · Title bar · Menu bar · Minimize · Maximize · Close · Move/Select pointer · Slider · Scroll bar · Resize pointers

Menu bar

Immediately below the Title bar in an application's window is a bar containing the names of its menus. Clicking on one of these will drop down a list of commands.

Scroll bars

These are present on the right side and bottom of the frame if the display contained by the window is too big to fit within it. The **Sliders** in the Scroll bars show you where your view is, relative to the overall display. Moving these allows you to view a different part of the display, (see *Scrolling*, **page 32**).

Window modes

All programs are displayed on screen in windows, and these can normally have three modes:

◆ Maximized - filling the whole screen;

◆ Minimized - not displayed, though still present as a button on the Task bar;

◆ Restore - adjustable in size and in position.

Take note

Some applications run in small, fixed-size windows, so Maximize and Restore do not apply to them.

Maximized

In **Restore** mode

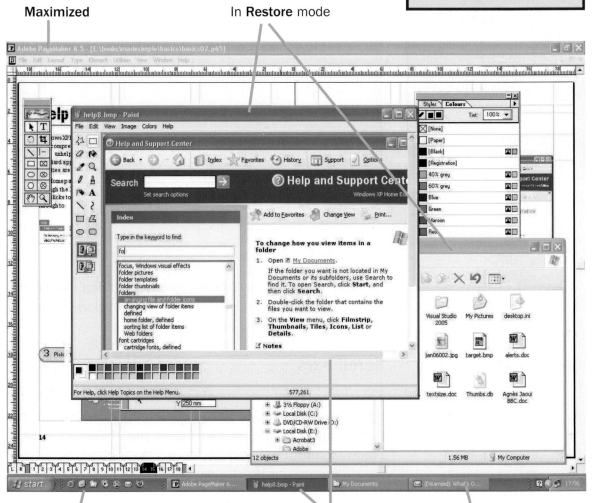

Clear the desk! Click here to minimize all windows and show the Desktop.

The current window is highlighted

Minimized – not visible except for this.

- ■ **To make a window full-screen**

  Click 🔲 or select **Maximize** from the Control menu

- ■ **To shrink a window to an icon**

  Click ▬ or select **Minimize** from the Control menu

- ■ **To restore a window to variable size**

  Click 🗗 or select **Restore** from the Control menu

Changing display modes

Clicking on the buttons in the top right corner of the frame is the simplest way to switch between **Maximize** and **Restore** modes, and to **Minimize** a window. If you prefer, it can be done using the Control menu.

The Control menu

Click the icon at the top left to open this. Options that don't apply at the time will be 'greyed out'. The menu here came from a variable size window. One from a full-screen window would have **Move**, **Size** and **Maximize** in grey.

Using the Taskbar

Click a program's button to bring its window to the top. Right-click the button to open its Control menu.

Right-click for the menu

Left-click to activate

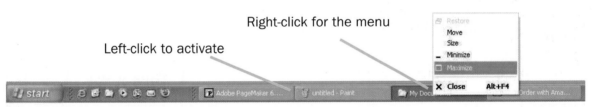

Keyboard control

[Alt]+[Space] opens the Control menu of an application.

[Alt]+[-] (minus) opens the Control menu of a document.

Minimized documents

When you minimize a document window, within an application, it shrinks to a tiny title bar, with just enough room for a name and the icons. Click **Maximize** or **Restore** to open it out again.

Restore   Maximize

Arranging windows

If you want to have two or more windows visible at the same time, you will have to arrange them on your Desktop. There are Windows tools that will do it for you, or you can do it yourself.

If you right-click the Taskbar, its menu has options to arrange the windows on the Desktop. Open it and you will see **Cascade Windows**, **Tile Windows Vertically** and **Tile Windows Horizontally**. Similar options are on the Window menu of most applications, though these only affect the layout *within* the programs.

Cascade places the windows overlapping with just the title bars of the back ones showing. You might just as well Maximize the current window, and use the Taskbar buttons to get to the rest.

Either of the Tile layouts can be the basis of a well-arranged Desktop.

1 **Maximize** or **Restore** the windows that you want to include in the layout. **Minimize** those that you will not be using actively.

2 Right-click the **Taskbar** to open its menu.

3 Select **Tile Windows Horizontally** or **Tile Windows Vertically**.

4 If you only want to work in one window at a time, **Maximize** it, and **Restore** it back into the arrangement when you have done.

Tip

If you want to adjust the balance of the layout, you can move and resize the windows.

Take note

The simplest way to switch to another open window is to click on its Taskbar button.

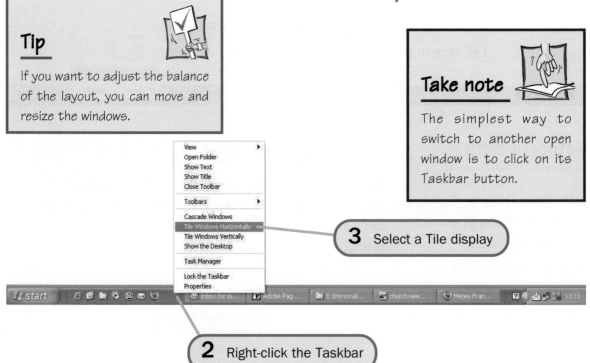

3 Select a Tile display

2 Right-click the Taskbar

Tile

Tip

Cascade works better than Tile on small screens.

Tile arranges open windows side by side (Vertically), or one above the other (Horizontally) – though with more than three windows, the tiling is in both directions. As the window frames take up space, the actual working area is significantly reduced. Obviously, larger, high-resolution screens are better for multi-window work, but even on a 1024 × 768 display you cannot do much serious typing in a tiled window.

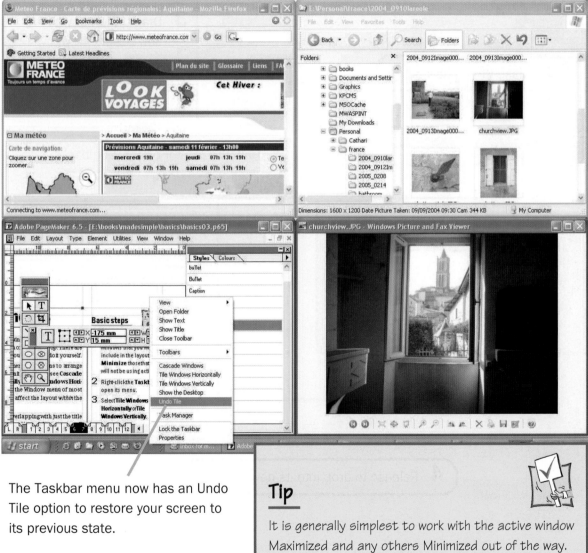

The Taskbar menu now has an Undo Tile option to restore your screen to its previous state.

Tip

It is generally simplest to work with the active window Maximized and any others Minimized out of the way.

29

Moving windows

When a window is in **Restore** mode – open but not full screen – it can be moved anywhere on the screen.

◆ If you are not careful it can be moved almost off the screen! Fortunately, at least a bit of the Title bar will still be visible, and that is the handle you need to grab to pull it back into view.

Basic steps

1 If the Title bar isn't highlighted, click on the window to make it the active one.

2 Point at the Title bar and hold the left button down.

3 Drag the window to its new position – you will only see a grey outline moving.

4 Release the button.

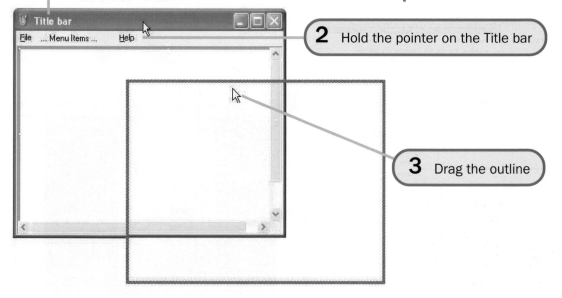

1 Make the window active

2 Hold the pointer on the Title bar

3 Drag the outline

4 Release to drop into its new position

Basic steps

1 Move the pointer to the edge or corner that you want to pull in or out.

2 When you see the double-headed arrow, hold down the left mouse button and drag the outline to the required size.

3 Release the button.

When a window is in Restore mode, you can change its size and shape by dragging the edges of the frame to new positions.

Combined with the moving facility, this lets you arrange your Desktop exactly the way you like it.

◆ The resize pointers only appear when the pointer is just on an edge, and they disappear again if you go too far. Practise! You'll soon get the knack of catching them.

You can drag any edge or corner

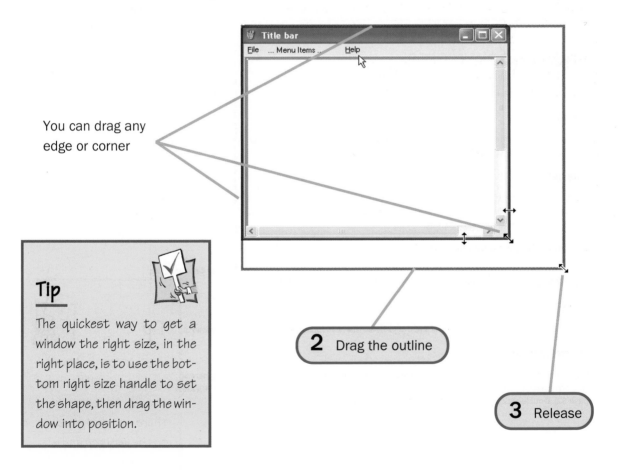

2 Drag the outline

3 Release

Tip

The quickest way to get a window the right size, in the right place, is to use the bottom right size handle to set the shape, then drag the window into position.

Scrolling

What you can see in a window is often only part of the story. The working area of the application may well be much larger. If there are scroll bars on the side and/or bottom of the window, this tells you that there is more material outside the frame. The scroll bars let you pull some of this material into view.

Sliders

The window frame

This is more than just a pretty border. It contains all the controls you need for adjusting the display.

Frame edge

This has a control system built into it. When a window is in Restore mode – i.e. smaller than full-screen – you can drag on the edge to make it larger or smaller (see *Changing the size*, page 37).

Title bar

This is to remind you of where you are – the title bar of the active application (the one you are using) is blue; the bars of other open applications are grey. The bar is also used for moving the window. Drag on this and the window moves (see *Moving windows*, page 36).

Maximize, Minimize and Restore

at any one time (see *Window modes*, page 32).

Close

One of several ways to close a window and the program that was running in it (see *Closing windows*, p...

Control menu icon

There is no set image for this icon, as every application has its own, but clicking on whatever is here w... the Control menu. This can be used for changing the screen mode or closing the window (see *Window...* page 32). Double-clicking this icon will close down the window.

Working area

Basic scrolls

- Drag the **slider** to scroll the view in the window. Drag straight along the bar or it won't work!

- Click an **arrow** ⌃ to edge the slider towards the arrow. Hold down for a slow continuous scroll.

- Click on the **bar** beside the Slider to make it jump towards the pointer.

Arrow buttons

Tip

If a window is blank – and you think there should be something there – push the sliders to the very top and left. That's where your work is likely to be.

Closing windows

- **Closing an active window**

1 Click ⊠ or press
[Alt]+[F4].

- **Closing from the Taskbar**

2 Right-click the program's
Taskbar button to get its
menu.

3 Select **Close**.

4 If you have forgotten to
save your work, take the
opportunity that is
offered to you.

When you close a window, you close down the program that was running inside it.

If you haven't saved your work, most programs will point this out and give you a chance to save before closing.

There are at least five different ways of closing. Here are the simplest three:

◆ If the window is in Maximized or Restore mode, click the close icon at the top right of the Title bar. (If your mouse control is not too good, you may well do this when you are trying to Maximize the window!)

◆ If the window has been Minimized onto the Taskbar, right-click on its button to open the Control menu and use **Close**.

◆ If you prefer working from keys, press **[Alt]+[F4]**.

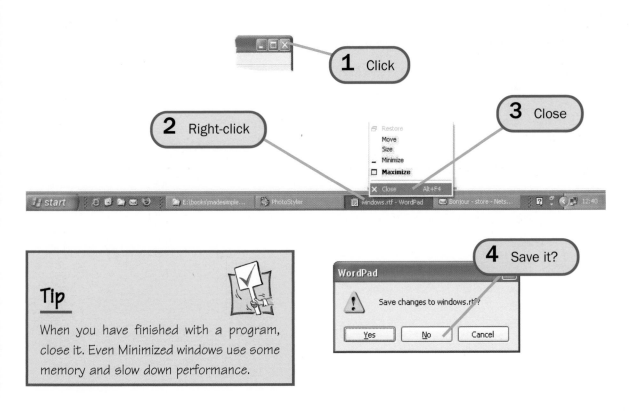

1 Click

3 Close

2 Right-click

4 Save it?

Tip

When you have finished with a program, close it. Even Minimized windows use some memory and slow down performance.

Exercises

1 Start up and log on to your PC, if necessary.

2 Run at least four applications – you can start the same application more than once if you like – the important thing is to have at least four windows open.

3 Arrange the windows in a Tile display. Minimize two or the windows, then re-Tile them.

4 Drag one of the windows into the centre and increase its size until it takes up around half of the screen space.

5 Select one of the minimized windows and maximize it from its Taskbar button.

6 Bring the half-size window (from 5) to the front.

7 Select and close one of the windows.

8 Arrange the windows in a Cascade display. Bring the rearmost one to the front and close it.

9 Resize and arrange the windows so that they are overlapping, but about three-quarters of each is visible.

10 Close all the windows.

3 Disks and folders

The faces of Explorer

Windows XP has one file management application, but with four very distinct faces. Whichever one you start from, it can be changed into any other by altering the display or by switching the focus between your computer, your network and the Internet.

Windows Explorer (page 40)

This has a dual display, with the folder structure on the left and the contents of the current folder on the right. It can access the folders in all of the drives attached to your computer, and any that may be accessible to you over a network. Windows Explorer is a good tool for moving files between folders.

My Computer (page 41)

In this mode, the folder structure display is replaced by a panel containing sets of commonly used tasks – the sets vary, depending upon what's selected at the time. When first opened it gives an overview of the components of your own system. You can then open another window to get a detailed look at folders in a drive, and continue opening further windows to go deeper into folders. My Computer only shows the contents of one folder, but you can have as many My Computer windows open as you need.

My Network Places

This is the same as My Computer, but opens with the focus on the networked machines.

Internet Explorer

This is the mode for exploring the Internet. The main differences are that it displays Web content and the toolbar has a slightly different selection of tools.

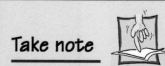

Take note

Which display you use for your file management is up to you. I prefer to see the folder structure for most jobs – certainly for organising files and folders – but use the simpler, My Computer display when I'm simply looking to see what's where or if I need two folders open at once to compare their contents.

Tip

The Desktop icon **My Documents** simply opens My Computer at the My Documents folder.

36

The jargon

- **Root** – the folder of the disk. All other folders branch off from the root.

- **Parent** – a folder that contains another.

- **Child** – a sub-folder of a Parent.

- **Branch** – the structure of sub-folders open off from a folder.

If you are going to work successfully with Windows – or any computer system – you must understand how its disk storage is organised, and how to manage files efficiently and safely. In this chapter, we will look at the filing system, working with folders and the screen displays of Explorer and My Computer. In later sections, we will cover managing files and looking after your disks.

Folders

The hard disks supplied on modern PCs are typically 10 gigabytes or larger – 1 gigabyte is 1 billion bytes and each byte can hold one character (or part of a number or of a graphic). That means that a typical hard disk can nearly to 2 billion words – enough for about 10,000 hefty novels! More to the point, if you were using it to store letters and reports, it could hold many, many thousands of them. Even if you are storing big audio or video files you are still going to get hundreds of them on the disk. It must be organised if you are ever to find your files.

Folders provide this organisation. They are containers in which related files can be placed to keep them together, and away from other files. A folder can also contain sub-folders – which can themselves be subdivided. You can think of the first level of folders as being sets of filing cabinets; the second level are drawers within the cabinets, and the next level divisions within the drawers. (And these could have subdividers – there is no limit to this.)

Don't just store all your files in My Documents – it will get terribly crowded! Have a separate folder for each type of file, or each area of work (or each user of the computer), subdividing as necessary, so that no folder holds more than a few dozen files.

Tip

When planning the folder structure, keep it simple. Too many folders within folders can make it hard to find files.

Paths

The structure of folders is often referred to as the **tree**. It starts at the **root**, which is the drive letter – C: for your main hard disk – and branches off from there.

A folder's position in the tree is described by its **path**. For most operations, you can identify a folder by clicking on it in a screen display, but now and then you will have to type its path. This should start at the drive letter and the root, and include every folder along the branch, with a backslash (\) between the names.

For example:

C:\DTP

C:\WORDPROC\LETTERS

When you want to know a path, look it up in the Explorer display and trace the branches down from the root.

Filenames

A filename has two parts – the name and an extension.

The **name** can be as long as you like, and include almost any characters – including spaces. But don't let the freedom go to your head. The longer the name, the greater the opportunity for typing errors. The most important thing to remember when naming a file is that the name must mean something to you, so that you can find it easily next time you come back to the job.

The **extension** can be from 0 to 3 characters, and is separated from the rest of the name by a dot. It is used to identify the nature of the file. Windows uses the extensions COM, EXE, SYS, INI, DLL to identify special files of its own – handle these with care!

Most applications also use their own special extensions. Word documents are marked with DOC; spreadsheet files are usually XLS; database files typically have DB extensions.

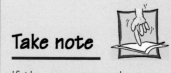

Take note

If there are several users, they will all have their own 'My Documents' folder set up by Windows XP – any new folders should be created within this.

Tip

Don't worry overmuch about remembering paths. When you want to access a file in an application, you will be taken to an **Open** panel in which you can select the drive, folder and file from a graphical display. Those that do not open this panel directly will have a [Browse...] button to open it.

If you are saving a file in a word-processor, spreadsheet or other application, and are asked for a filename, you normally only have to give the first part. The application will take care of the extension. If you do need to give an extension, make it meaningful. BAK is a good extension for backup files; TXT for text files.

When an application asks you for a filename - and the file is in the *current* folder - type in the name and extension only. If the file is in *another* folder, type in the path, a backslash separator and then the filename.

For example:

MYFILE.DOC

C:\WORPROC\REPORTS\MAY25.TXT

A:\MYFILE.BAK

Browse dialog boxes from two applications. In some older applications *folders* are called *directories*.

Windows Explorer

In the Explorer window, the main working area is split, with folders in the Explorer bar, and the contents on the right.

The **Folder List** may show the disk drives and first level of folders only, but folders can be expanded to show the sub-folders (see *Expanding folders*, **page 45**).

The **Contents** area shows the files and sub-folders in the currently selected folder. These can be displayed as thumb-nails, tiles, icons or with details of the file's size, type and date it was last modified (see *Arranging files*, **page 54**).

The **Status bar** shows information about the selected file(s) or folders.

The **Toolbar** has the buttons for the most commonly-used commands. Other can be added, if desired.

The **Explorer bar** can also be used to display Common Tasks (see **page 40**), Search (see **page 62**), Favorites or History (when used online – not covered in this book).

Basic steps

■ **Starting Explorer**

1 Click ⟦ start ⟧.

2 Point to **All Programs** then to **Accessories**.

3 Click **Windows Explorer**.

4 Click on a folder's icon 🗀 or its name to open it and display its contents.

Take note

See page 45 to read about the ⊞ and ⊟ icons in the Folders list.

Contents – here shown in **Icon view**

Click to close the Explorer bar

Explorer bar, displaying the Folder List

Current folder

First level folder

Sub-folder

Status bar

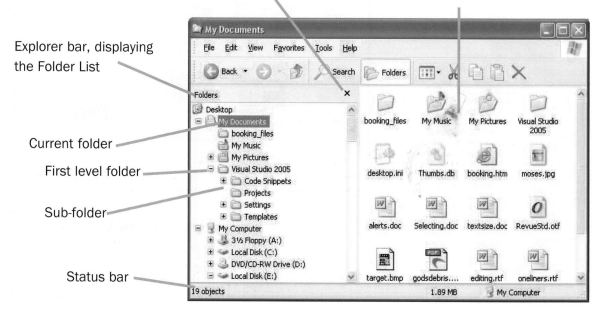

My Computer

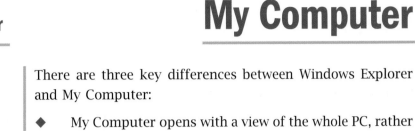

Back ▾ | Go to folder you last looked at

○ ▾ | Go to next folder

Up to parent folder

Search | Search for files

Folders | Toggle Folder List and Common Tasks

▦ ▾ | Alternative views

✂ | Cut = copy and delete

Copy files into Clipboard

Paste from Clipboard

✕ | Delete

There are three key differences between Windows Explorer and My Computer:

◆ My Computer opens with a view of the whole PC, rather than starting in *My Documents*.

◆ Instead of the Folder List, the Explorer bar shows **Common Tasks** - these vary, depending upon what is selected in the Contents pane.

◆ The Status bar is turned off by default.

Any or all of these can be changed.

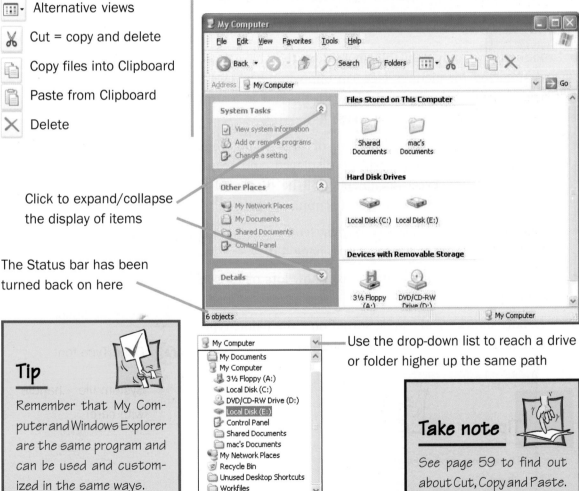

Click to expand/collapse the display of items

The Status bar has been turned back on here

Use the drop-down list to reach a drive or folder higher up the same path

Tip

Remember that My Computer and Windows Explorer are the same program and can be used and customized in the same ways.

Take note

See page 59 to find out about Cut, Copy and Paste.

Display options

The display options can be set from the View menu and the Views button. These options can be set at any time, and can be different for different folders. There are two areas of choice.

Which toolbars to you want?

◆ The **Standard** is pretty well essential.

◆ The **Address** is useful. Its drop-down outline of the folder structure offers a quick way to move between drives.

◆ The **Links** carries quick links to selected web sites.

Alternative views

◆ **Filmstrip** is only available in folders that have been customized for pictures (see Tip opposite). It shows a large image of the selected file, with the rest in a strip across the bottom (example, **page 44**).

◆ **Thumbnails** show little previews of files, if possible. Graphics and web pages will be displayed, and Word, PowerPoint and Excel documents will be displayed if they were saved with a preview (example, **page 44**).

◆ **Tiles** shows a large, easy to recognise icon, accompanied by key details of the file (example, **page 43**).

◆ **Icons** (example, **page 40**) and **List** show lots of files in little space.

◆ **Details** shows – and can be sorted on – the name, type, size and date of files (example, **page 45**).

Tip

There's more on arranging files in Chapter 4.

Basic steps

- ■ **Displaying toolbars**
- **1** Open the **View** menu.
- **2** Point to **Toolbars** then click on a toolbar to turn it on or off.
- ■ **Icons and lists**
- **3** Open the **View** menu.

Or

- **4** Click .
- **5** Choose a view.

Common file icons

 Bitmap image

 Text

Word document

 Web page

 PDF file

Excel workbook

 Open Type font

 System file – handle with care!

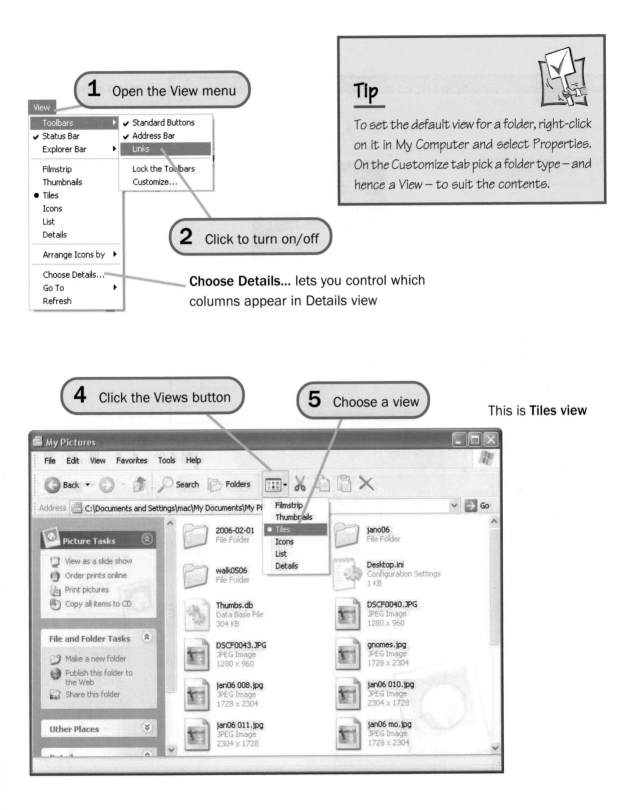

1 Open the View menu

View
Toolbars ▶	✔ Standard Buttons
✔ Status Bar	✔ Address Bar
Explorer Bar ▶	Links
	Lock the Toolbars
Filmstrip	Customize...
Thumbnails	
● Tiles	
Icons	
List	
Details	
Arrange Icons by ▶	
Choose Details...	
Go To ▶	
Refresh	

2 Click to turn on/off

Choose Details... lets you control which columns appear in Details view

Tip

To set the default view for a folder, right-click on it in My Computer and select Properties. On the Customize tab pick a folder type – and hence a View – to suit the contents.

4 Click the Views button

5 Choose a view

This is **Tiles view**

My Pictures

File   Edit   View   Favorites   Tools   Help

Back ▾   Search   Folders   ▥ ▾   ✂ 🗎 📋 ✕

Address 🖻 C:\Documents and Settings\mac\My Documents\My Pi   ⌄   ➡ Go

| Filmstrip |
| Thumbnails |
| ● Tiles |
| Icons |
| List |
| Details |

Picture Tasks
- View as a slide show
- Order prints online
- Print pictures
- Copy all items to CD

File and Folder Tasks
- Make a new folder
- Publish this folder to the Web
- Share this folder

Other Places

2006-02-01
File Folder

walk0506
File Folder

Thumbs.db
Data Base File
304 KB

DSCF0043.JPG
JPEG Image
1280 x 960

jan06 008.jpg
JPEG Image
1728 x 2304

jan06 011.jpg
JPEG Image
2304 x 1728

jano06
File Folder

Desktop.ini
Configuration Settings
1 KB

DSCF0040.JPG
JPEG Image
1280 x 960

gnomes.jpg
JPEG Image
1728 x 2304

jan06 010.jpg
JPEG Image
2304 x 1728

jan06 mo.jpg
JPEG Image
1728 x 2304

Filmstrip view
The size of the main image depends upon the size of the window

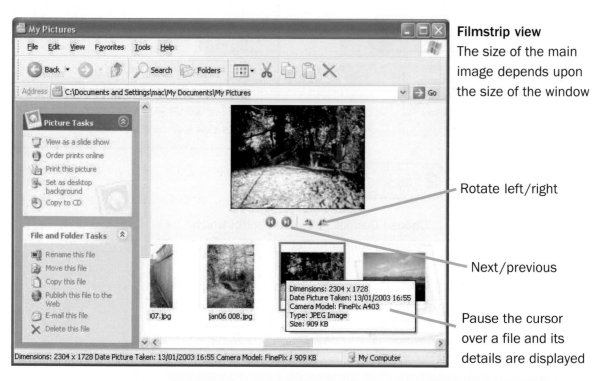

Rotate left/right

Next/previous

Pause the cursor over a file and its details are displayed

Thumbnail view
Good for images and web pages

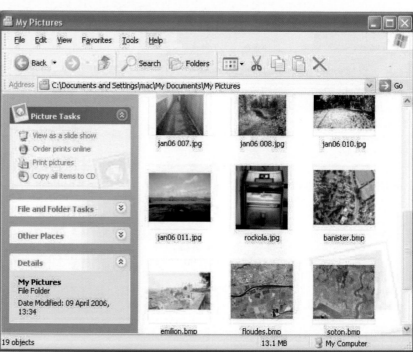

Expanding folders

Basic steps

- **To expand a folder**

1 Click **+** by its name.

2 Click **+** by any sub-folders if you want to fully expand the whole branching set.

- **To collapse a folder**

3 Click **−** by its name.

q **To collapse a whole branch**

4 Click **−** by the folder at the top of the branched set.

The *Folders* structure can be shown in outline form, or with some or all of its branches shown in full. The best display is always the simplest one that will show you all you need. This usually means that most of the structure is collapsed back to its first level of main folders, with one or two branches expanded to show particular sub-folders. It is sometimes worth expanding the whole lot, just to get an idea of the overall structure and to see how sub-folders fit together.

If a folder has sub-folders, it will have a symbol beside it.

+   has sub-folders, and can be expanded

−   sub-folders displayed and can be collapsed.

1 Expand folder

4 Collapse whole set

3 Collapse folder

2 Expand sub-folder

Illustrator 9.0 window:

File | Edit | View | Favorites | Tools | Help

Back • | Search | Folders

Address: C:\Program Files\Adobe\Illustrator 9.0

Folders:
- Kpcms
- madesimple
- MSOCache
- Program Files
  - Adobe
    - Acrobat 7.0
    - Illustrator 9.0
      - Action Sets
      - Plug-ins
        - Extensions
        - Illustrator Filters
        - Illustrator Formal
        - Photoshop Forma
        - Text Filters
        - Tools
      - Required
      - Settings

Name	Size	Type
Action Sets		File Folder
Plug-ins		File Folder
Required		File Folder
Settings		File Folder
System		File Folder
(c)Adobe.txt	23 KB	Text Document
ACE.dll	428 KB	Application Ext
AGM.dll	1,672 KB	Application Ext
AGM.rsl	60 KB	PageMaker Re:
BIB.dll	100 KB	Application Ext
bookmark.htm	0 KB	HTML Document
coldware.dll	44 KB	Application Ext
CoolType.dll	1,176 KB	Application Ext
Ha311w32.dll	362 KB	Application Ext
Illustrator.exe	4,125 KB	Application
MPS.dll	3,372 KB	Application Ext
OPP.dll	68 KB	Application Ext

24 objects (Disk free space: 30.0 GB) | 13.1 MB | My Computer

Creating a folder

Organised people set up their folders before they need them, so that they have places to store their letters, reports, memos, notes and whatever, when they start to write them on their system. They have a clear idea of the structure that they want, and create their folders at the right branches.

How you organise your folders is entirely up to you, but don't have too many levels of sub-folders – it gets confusing. Create the main folders in My Documents, or at the C: drive if you are the PC's only user, and aim for no more than two levels of sub-folders within these. It's a pain having to work through four or five levels to reach stuff!

1 Select the folder that will be the parent of your new one, or the root if you want a new first-level folder.

2 Open the **File** menu and point to **New** then select **Folder**.

3 Replace 'New Folder' with a new name – any length, any characters, as with filenames.

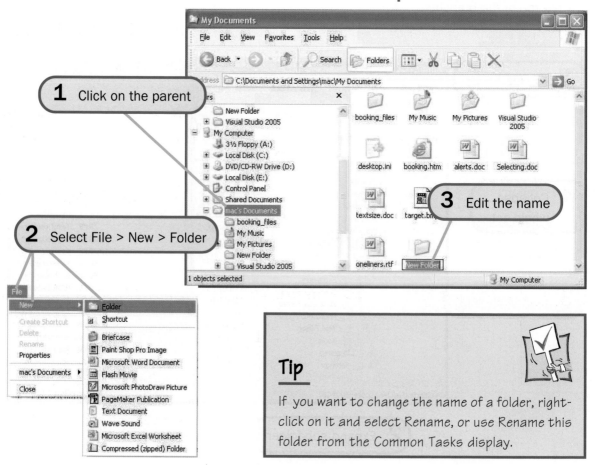

1 Click on the parent

2 Select File > New > Folder

3 Edit the name

Tip

If you want to change the name of a folder, right-click on it and select Rename, or use Rename this folder from the Common Tasks display.

Moving folders

1 Arrange the display so that you can see the folder you want to move and the place it has to move to.

2 Drag the folder to its new position – the highlight will show you which one is currently selected.

Those of us who are less organised set up our new folders when the old ones get so full that it is difficult to find things. Nor do we always create them in the most suitable place in the tree. Fortunately, Windows XP caters for us too. Files can easily be moved from one folder to another (see *Moving and copying*, **page 58**), and folders can easily be moved to new places on the tree.

Here, *WebPix* is being moved from within *My Documents* folder into *Shared Documents*, so that others can access it.

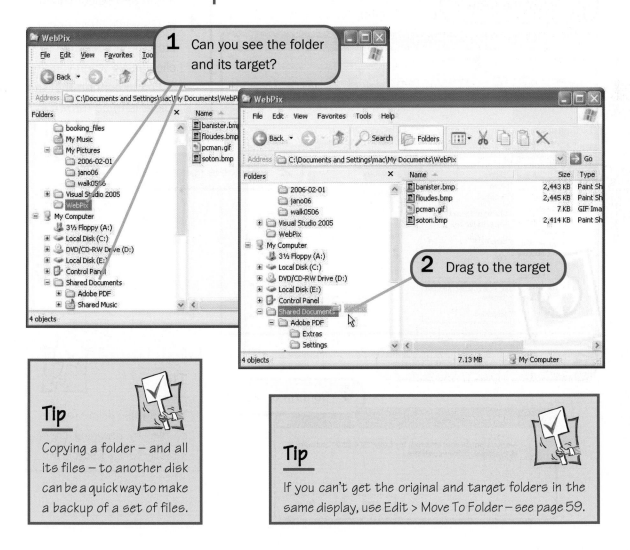

1 Can you see the folder and its target?

2 Drag to the target

Tip

Copying a folder – and all its files – to another disk can be a quick way to make a backup of a set of files.

Tip

If you can't get the original and target folders in the same display, use Edit > Move To Folder – see page 59.

Deleting folders

This is not something you will do every day, for deleting a folder also deletes its files, and files are usually precious things. But we all acquire programs we don't need, keep files long past their use-by dates, and sometimes create unnecessary folders.

◆ Don't worry about accidental deletions – folders deleted from your hard disk can be restored thanks to the Recycle Bin (see **page 61**).

(see **page 61**)

1 Select the folder.

2 Check the files list. Are there any there? Do you want any of them? No, then carry on.

3 Right-click on the folder to open the context menu or open the **File** menu and select **Delete**.

4 If necessary, you can stop the process by clicking **No** when you are asked to confirm that the folder is to be thrown in the Bin.

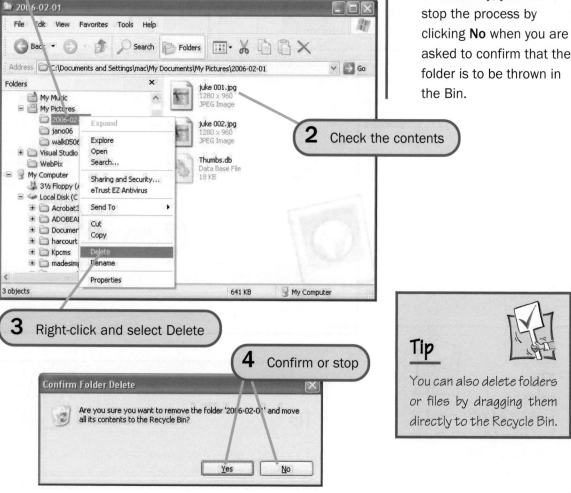

1 Select the folder

2 Check the contents

3 Right-click and select Delete

4 Confirm or stop

Tip

You can also delete folders or files by dragging them directly to the Recycle Bin.

Folder Options

1 Run My Computer (or Windows Explorer).

2 From the **Tools** menu select **Folder Options...**

3 On the **General** tab, click to set the **Tasks**, **Browse folders** and **Click items** options.

4 If you opt for single-click opening, you must choose how items are to be underlined.

5 Leave the dialog box open – there's more...

Many aspects of Windows can be customized, and My Computer is no exception. You can adjust the way My Computer behaves, and the way that it displays files. Here are the key options which you can set – there are others which you might like to explore later.

General options

◆ The Common Tasks display, on the left of the window, can be turned off if not wanted. It was not present in earlier version of Windows, which is why this option is labelled 'Use Windows classic folders'.

◆ When you open a folder, it can open in the same My Computer window or in a new one.

◆ You can set it so that a single click opens an item (as on a Web page), or so that a single click selects it, and a double-click is needed to open it (as in earlier Windows).

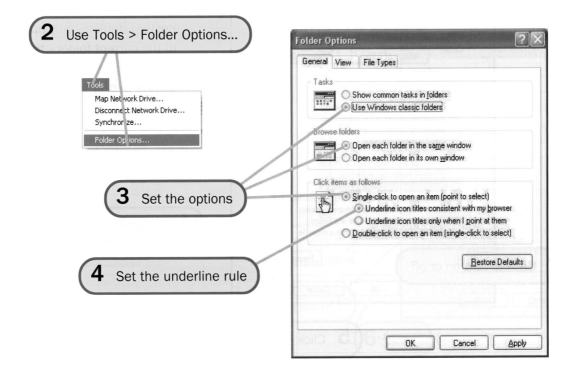

2 Use Tools > Folder Options...

3 Set the options

4 Set the underline rule

Tools
Map Network Drive...
Disconnect Network Drive...
Synchronize...
Folder Options...

Folder Options

General | View | File Types

Tasks
○ Show common tasks in folders
◉ Use Windows classic folders

Browse folders
◉ Open each folder in the same window
○ Open each folder in its own window

Click items as follows
◉ Single-click to open an item (point to select)
  ◉ Underline icon titles consistent with my browser
  ○ Underline icon titles only when I point at them
○ Double-click to open an item (single-click to select)

Restore Defaults

OK | Cancel | Apply

Exercises

1 Start up and log on to your PC, if necessary.

2 Start Windows Explorer (or My Computer and turn on the Folders list). In *My Documents*, create three new folders called *Work*, *Study* and *Leisure*.

3 Within *Study*, create a subfolder called *Exam Practice*.

4 Delete the folder *Leisure* – you don't have time for that!

5 Plan your folder structure – what do you use your PC for? What sort of files will you want to store and under what headings? Identify the main areas, then think how you might best subdivide them.

6 Rename the *Work* and *Study* folders to suit two of your main areas, and *Exam Practice* to suit a subdivision of its folder.

7 Create the other new folders that you need to set up a basic structure for storing your files.

Take note

You can create, rename and delete folders at any time, to meet your changing needs for storage.

4 Managing files

Arranging files

Unless you specify otherwise, folders and files are listed in alphabetical order. Most of the time this works fine, but when you are moving or copying files, or hunting for them, other arrangements can be more convenient.

Basic steps

1 Open the **View** menu and point to **Arrange Icons by.**

2 Select **Name, Size, Type,** or **Modified** (date).

■ **Details View**

3 Open the **View** menu and select **Details.**

4 To sort by **Name, Size, Type** or **Date**, click on the column header. Click again to sort into reverse order.

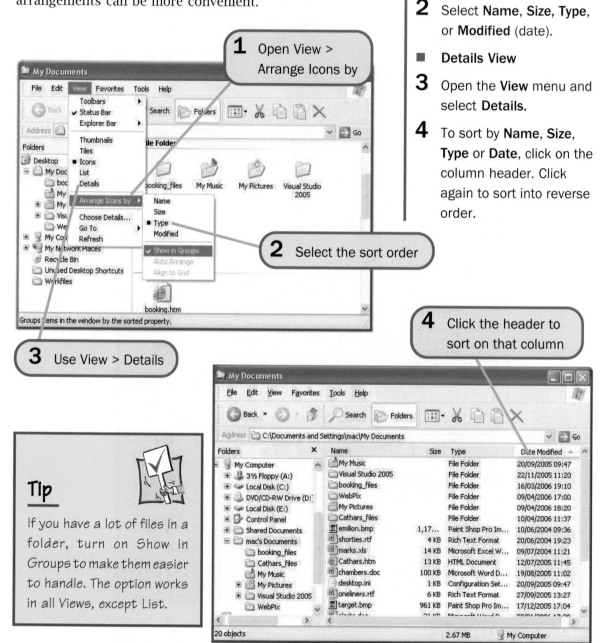

> **1** Open View > Arrange Icons by

> **2** Select the sort order

> **3** Use View > Details

> **4** Click the header to sort on that column

Tip

If you have a lot of files in a folder, turn on Show in Groups to make them easier to handle. The option works in all Views, except List.

Improving visibility

Basic steps

- **Adjusting details**

1 Point the cursor at the
   dividing line between two
   field headings.

2 When the cursor changes
   to ↔, drag to change
   the width of the field on
   its left.

- **Adjusting the split**

3 Point anywhere on the
   bar between the panes
   to get the ↔ cursor,
   then drag the dividing
   bar to adjust the relative
   size of the panes.

The amount of information in a My Computer or Windows Explorer display can vary greatly, depending upon the number of items in a folder and the display style. You should be able to adjust the display so that you can see things properly.

As well as being able to set the overall size of the window, you can also adjust the width of each field in a Details display, and the split between the Folders and Contents panes of Explorer.

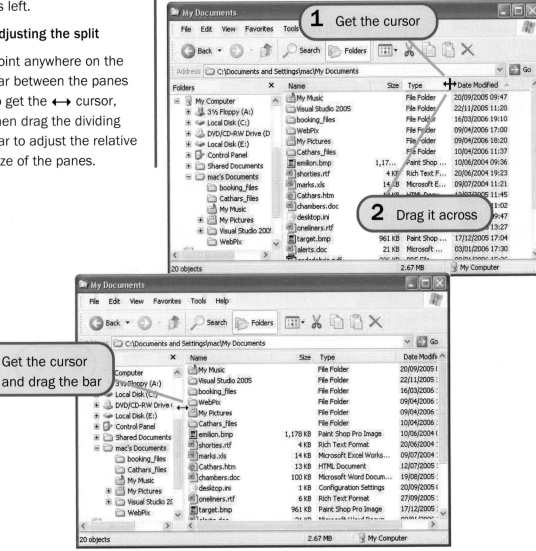

55

Selecting sets of files

You can easily select one file by clicking on it, but you can also select sets of files. This is useful when you want to back up a day's work by copying the new files to a floppy, or move a set from one folder to another or delete a load of unwanted files.

You can select:

◆ a block of adjacent files;

◆ a scattered set;

◆ the whole folder-full.

The same techniques work with all display styles.

Basic steps

■ **To select a block using the mouse**

1 Point to one corner of the block and click.

2 Drag an outline onto the ones you want.

■ **[Shift] selecting**

3 Click on the file at one end of the block.

4 If necessary, scroll the window to bring the other end into view.

5 Hold [Shift].

6 Click on the far end file.

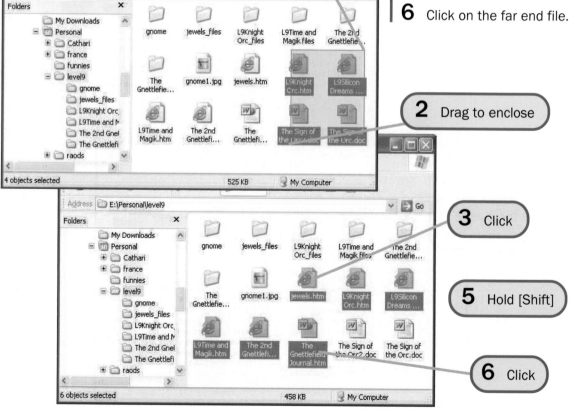

56

Basic steps

- **To select scattered files**

1 Click on any one of the files you want.

2 Hold [**Control**] and click each of the other files.

- You can deselect any file by clicking on it a second time.

- **To select all the files**

3 Open the **Edit** menu.

4 Choose **Select All**.

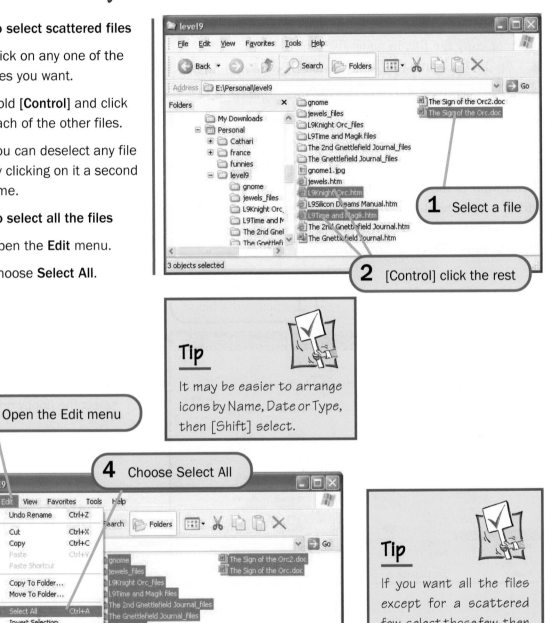

1 Select a file

2 [Control] click the rest

3 Open the Edit menu

4 Choose Select All

Tip

It may be easier to arrange icons by Name, Date or Type, then [Shift] select.

Tip

If you want all the files except for a scattered few, select those few, then use Edit > Invert Selection to deselect them and select the others.

Moving and copying

When you drag a file from one place to another, it will either move or copy the file. In general:

◆   It is a **move** if you drag to somewhere *on the same disk*.

◆   It is a **copy** if you drag the file *to a different disk*.

When you are dragging files within a disk, you are usually moving to reorganise your storage; and copying is most commonly used to create a safe backup on a separate disk.

If you want to move a file from one disk to another, or copy within a disk, hold down the right mouse button while you drag. A menu will appear when you reach the target folder. You can select **Move** or **Copy** from there.

Basic steps

1   Select the file(s).

2   Scroll the **Folders** list so that you can see the target folder – don't click on it!

3   Point to any one of the selected files and drag to the target.

Or

4   Hold down the right mouse button while you drag then select **Move** or **Copy**.

■   **Quick copy to a floppy**

5   Right-click on the file to open its context menu, point to **Send To** and select the floppy drive.

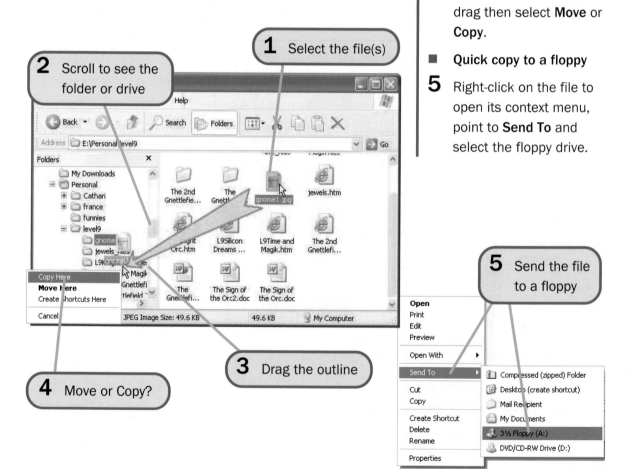

1   Select the file(s)

2   Scroll to see the folder or drive

4   Move or Copy?

3   Drag the outline

5   Send the file to a floppy

Move To Folder/Copy To Folder

1 Select the file(s).

2 Open the **Edit** menu and select **Copy To** or **Move To Folder**.

3 Select the target drive or folder.

4 Click **Move** or **Copy**.

If you are having difficulty arranging the Explorer display so that you can see the source files and the target folder, the simplest approach is to use the **Move To Folder** or **Copy To Folder** commands. These let you pick the target folder through a dialog box.

Tip

If you like this method of managing files, you can add Copy To and Move To buttons to the toolbar.

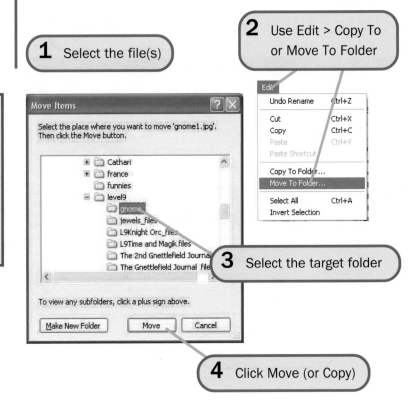

1 Select the file(s)

2 Use Edit > Copy To or Move To Folder

3 Select the target folder

4 Click Move (or Copy)

Cut and Paste

Windows XP allows you to move and copy files and folders – or any other data, through an area of memory called the Clipboard.

Cut, **Copy** and **Paste** are on the **Edit** menu of all Windows applications.

Copy stores a copy of the file or folder in the Clipboard.

Cut removes the original file, storing a copy in the Clipboard.

Paste puts a copy of the stored file into the current folder.

Deleting files

Thanks to the Recycle Bin, deleting files is no longer the dangerous occupation that it used to be – up to a point! Anything that you delete from the hard disk goes first into the Bin, from which it can easily be recovered. Floppies are different. If you delete a file from a floppy it really does get wiped out!

Basic steps

1 Select the file, or group of files.

2 Drag them to the **Recycle Bin** on the Desktop or in Explorer.

or

3 Press [**Delete**].

4 At the **Confirm** prompt, click **Yes** or **No** to confirm or stop the deletion.

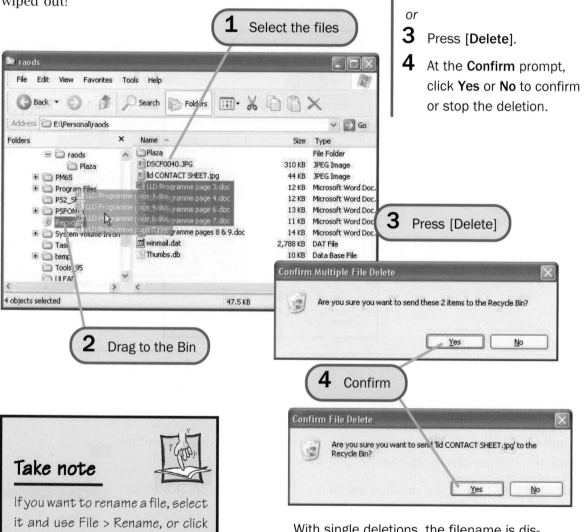

1 Select the files

3 Press [Delete]

2 Drag to the Bin

4 Confirm

With single deletions, the filename is displayed; with multiple deletions you just get the number of selected files.

Take note

If you want to rename a file, select it and use File > Rename, or click twice, separately, on the filename to highlight it. The name can then be edited or retyped.

Basic steps

1 Open the Recycle Bin from the icon on the Desktop or from Windows Explorer.

2 Select the files that were deleted by mistake – the **Original Location** field shows you where they were.

3 Right-click for the context menu and select **Restore** or click **Restore the selected items** in the common tasks.

Tip

Files sent to the Recycle Bin stay there until you empty it. Do this regularly, to free up disk space. Check that there is nothing that you want (Restore any files if necessary) then use File > Empty Recycle Bin.

Recycle Bin

The Recycle Bin

This is a wonderful feature, especially for those of us given to making instant decisions that we later regret. Until you empty the Bin, any 'deleted' files and folders can be instantly restored – and if the folder that they were stored in has also been deleted, that is re-created first, so things go back into their proper place.

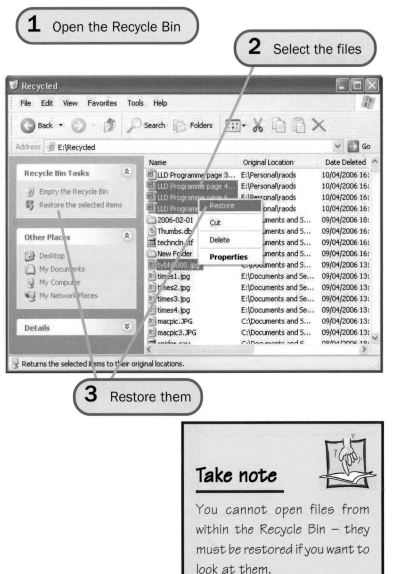

1 Open the Recycle Bin

2 Select the files

3 Restore them

Take note

You cannot open files from within the Recycle Bin – they must be restored if you want to look at them.

Finding files

If you are well organised, have a clear and logical structure of folders and consistently store files in their proper places, you should rarely need this facility. However, if you are like me, you will be grateful for it. You can find files by name, type, age, size or contents.

Partial names and wildcards

If you type part of a name into the name box, the Search will track down any file with those characters anywhere in the name.

e.g. '**DOC**' will find 'My **Doc**uments', 'Letter to **doc**tor', and all Word files with a **.DOC** extension.

If you know the start of the name and the extension, fill the gap with the wildcard ***.** (include the dot!)

e.g. **REP*.TXT** will find '**REP**ORT MAY 15**.TXT**', '**REP**LY TO IRS**.TXT**' and similar files.

1   In **My Computer** or **Windows Explorer**, click **Search**.

2   Select **All files or folders**.

3   Type as much of the name as you know into the **Name** slot.

4   If the file can be identified by a **word or phrase**, enter it.

5   Select the drive from the **Look in** list.

3 Type (part of) the name

4 Enter a word or phrase?

5 Set where to look

Search Results

File   Edit   View   Favorites   Tools   Help

Back   Search   Folders

Search Companion   ✕   To start your search, follow the instructions in the left pane.

Search by any or all of the criteria below.

All or part of the file name:
car park

A word or phrase in the file:

Look in:
Local Disk (E:)

When was it modified?   ⊗

What size is it?   ⊗

More advanced options   ⊗

Back   Search

0 objects

6 If you want to narrow the search, you can define **when it was modified**, its **size** and other **advanced options**, including type. Click ⌄ to open an option area and give any known details.

7 Click ⌊ Search ⌋.

8 Double-click the file to run it or to open it with its linked program.

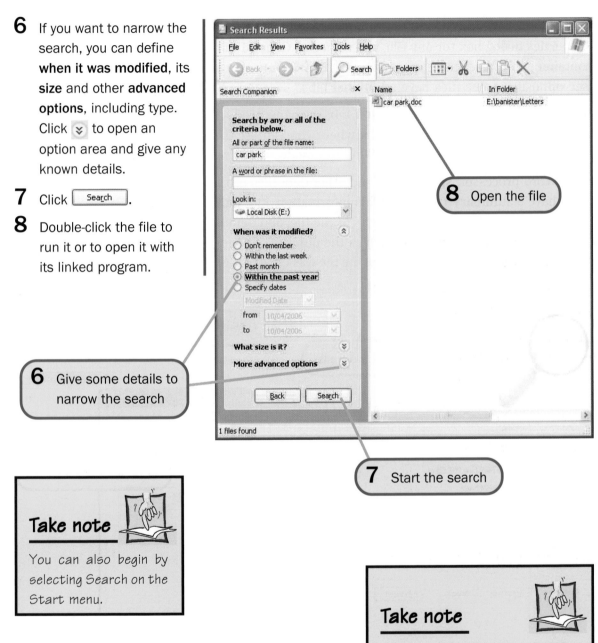

8 Open the file

6 Give some details to narrow the search

7 Start the search

Take note

You can also begin by selecting Search on the Start menu.

Take note

You can print, delete and otherwise manage a found file through options on the File menu.

Properties

Everything in Windows XP has Properties. If you open the **Properties** dialog box for any file, you will see a **General** tab, containing information about the file and its **Attribute** status (see opposite). Some files have additional tabs.

◆ Program files may have **Version** tabs carrying product details, and **Compatibility** tabs where you can set the program to run in an earlier Windows mode;

◆ Word-processor, spreadsheet and other data files often have a **Summary** tab. This holds information added by the user to describe the contents of the file, and details added by the application, such as the number of pages and words, and the dates when the file was created, last modified or accessed.

Basic steps

1 Right-click the file and select **Properties** from the short menu.

2 Read the file's details.

3 Click the tab names to open the other tabs.

4 Click  or ⊠ to close.

Open
New
Print
eTrust EZ Antivirus
Open With...
Send To ▶
Cut
Copy
Create Shortcut
Delete
Rename
Properties

1 Open Properties

2 See the details

pdfeditor.exe Properties

General | Version | Compatibility | Summary

🔲 pdfeditor.exe

Type of file: Application
Description: Jaws PDF Editor

Location: C:\Program Files\Jaws PDF Editor
Size: 276 KB (282,624 bytes)
Size on disk: 276 KB (282,624 bytes)

Created: 21 September 2005, 16:41:56
Modified: 12 September 2002, 21:37:06
Accessed: 10 April 2006, 22:29:46

Attributes: ☐ Read-only ☐ Hidden [Advanced...]

[OK] [Cancel] [Apply]

3 Look at other tabs

pdfeditor.exe Properties [?][X]

General | Version | **Compatibility** | Summary

If you have problems with this program and it worked correctly on an earlier version of Windows, select the compatibility mode that matches that earlier version.

Compatibility mode
☑ Run this program in compatibility mode for:
Windows 98 / Windows Me ▾

Display settings
☑ Run in 256 colors
☐ Run in 640 x 480 screen resolution
☐ Disable visual themes

Input settings
☐ Turn off advanced text services for this program

Learn more about program compatibility.

[OK] [Cancel] [Apply]

4 Click OK

Changing file attributes

1 Select the file(s) and open the **Properties** dialog box.

2 Click the **Read-only** checkbox to set or to remove the tick.

3 Click ☐ OK ☐.

Files have a number of *attributes*, and the key one of these is the **Read Only** protection. If this is turned on the file cannot be changed – or rather, you can open it and edit it, but you will not be able to save the changes. It is used to protect the file from accidental alteration, but this also get turned on when a file is saved to a CD (because you cannot resave a file on a CD). If you copy a file from a CD, you need to turn Read Only off if you want to edit it.

◆ You can change the attributes of several files at once if you need to.

---

marks.xls Properties [?][X]

General | Custom | Summary

 marks.xls

Type of file: Microsoft Excel Worksheet

Opens with: Microsoft Office Excel [Change...]

Location: C:\Documents and Settings\mac\My Documents

Size: 13.5 KB (13,824 bytes)

Size on disk: 16.0 KB (16,384 bytes)

Created: 09 July 2004, 11:21:22

Modified: 09 July 2004, 11:21:24

Accessed: 10 April 2006, 22:29:03

Attributes: ☑ Read-only ☐ Hidden [Advanced...]

[OK] [Cancel] [Apply]

2 Protect from changes?

Hidden files are not normally displayed in Windows Explorer – it helps to protect them from being moved or deleted

3 Click OK

The Advanced attributes are largely used to control how backups are done – they are best left alone.

Tip

If an older application does not work reliably in XP, try running it in the appropriate compatibility mode.

Renaming a file

Files can be renamed at any time. Renaming may be needed to replace the names that had been allocated by a program, e.g. when importing pictures from a camera or scanner. At other times you may want to rename a file to make it easier to identify its contents.

1 Right-click and select Rename

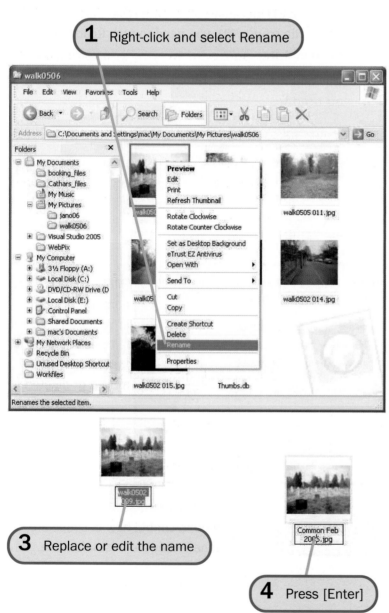

3 Replace or edit the name

4 Press [Enter]

Basic steps

1 Right-click the file and select **Rename** from the short menu.

Or

2 Select the file and press [**F2**].

3 The name will be high-lighted ready for editing. Start typing to replace it with the new name or click into it to delete or edit part of the name.

4 Press [**Enter**].

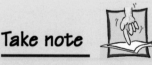

Take note

When renaming a file, you normally only change the first part of the name – not the extension, as this identifies the file type. If you change the extension, you are likely to confuse Windows. And remember that if the extension is not hidden, it will be selected with the rest of the name when you start editing. It is very easy to delete the extension by mistake.

File compression

Data is generally organised in files in whichever way best suits its application. This is often not the most compact way it can be stored, but that doesn't matter most of the time as storage space is rarely a problem on modern PCs. The size of files – and the amount of wasted space in them – may well matter when you are backing up, or copying files onto floppies, or uploading files onto a web site or sending them via e-mail.

1 Select the files and right-click on one of them.

2 Point to **Send To** and select **Compressed (zipped) Folder**.

Some types of files can be compressed more than others. Bitmaps (.bmp) typically compress down to 10% or less of their unpacked size and Word documents down to around 20%; text files – which have little waste to start with – and those graphics formats with built-in compression are not reduced much.

3 A message box will appear to show you the compression in progress. When it has finished there will be a new file with a .zip extension.

You can get compression software, such as WinZip, but Windows XP has the same technology embedded in Explorer.

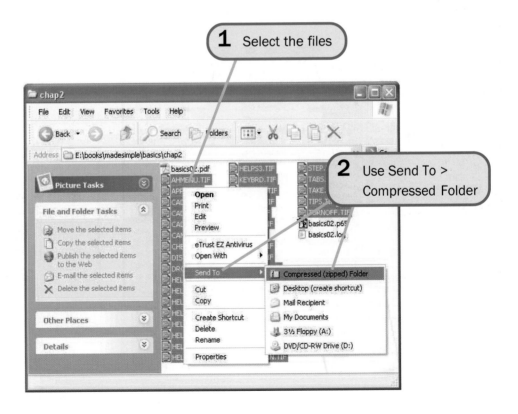

Extracting files

A zipped folder can be opened in almost the same way as an ordinary folder. Files in a zipped folder can be copied, moved, deleted and opened just as they can from a normal folder – with a couple of exceptions. The key one is this:

◆ If you edit a compressed file, you cannot save it back into the zipped folder. If you need to get an edited version back in, save it elsewhere then copy it in.

In general, it is best to extract files into another – ordinary – folder, before you do any work on them.

Basic steps

■ **To extract selected files**

1 Double-click on the zip folder to open it.

2 Select the files.

3 Use the **Copy** command in the **Folder Tasks** display, or from the right-click menu.

■ **To extract all the files**

4 Open the zip folder.

5 Use the **Extract All...** command from the **File** menu or in the **Folder Tasks** display.

5 Use Extract all files

2 Select the files

```
APPLY.zip
File  Edit  View  Favorites  Tools  Help
Back  ▼  ○  ▾  🔍 Search  📁 Folders  ▦▾  ✂ 📋 📋 ✕
Address  E:\books\madesimple\basics\chap2\APPLY.zip            ▼  → Go

Folder Tasks        ⊗        Name ▲        Type          Packe...  Has ...  Size ▲
                              AHMENU.TIF    Microsoft Offi...  1 KB    No    1 KB
  Extract all files           APPLY.TIF     Microsoft Offi...  1 KB    No    11 KB
                              CAD.TIF       Microsoft Offi...  63 KB   No    245 KB
File and Folder Tasks  ⊗      CAD1.TIF      Microsoft Offi...  1 KB    No    12 KB
                              CAD2.TIF      Microsoft Offi...  28 KB   No    169 KB
  Move the selected items     CANCEL.TIF    Microsoft Offi...  1 KB    No    11 KB
  Copy the selected items     CHECKS.TIF    Microsoft Offi...  3 KB    No    20 KB
  Publish the selected items  DISPLAY.TIF   Microsoft Offi...  2 KB    No    13 KB
  to the Web                  DROPDOWN.TIF  Microsoft Offi...  7 KB    No    59 KB
  Delete the selected items   HELP10.TIF    Microsoft Offi...  168 KB  No    361 KB
                              HELP8.TIF     Microsoft Offi...  166 KB  No    364 KB
                              HELP9.TIF     Microsoft Offi...  65 KB   No    237 KB
Other Places        ⊗         HELPGO.TIF    Microsoft Offi...  3 KB    No    6 KB
                              HELPMENU.TIF  Microsoft Offi...  5 KB    No    51 KB
Details             ⊗         HELPQ.TIF     Microsoft Offi...  2 KB    No    5 KB
                              HELPS1A.TIF   Microsoft Offi...  150 KB  No    343 KB
                              HELPS2.TIF    Microsoft Offi...  155 KB  No    352 KB ▼
3 objects selected
```

3 Use the Copy command

Take note

If you drag a file into a compressed folder, it is copied – not moved.

Basic steps

1 If the program has a Start menu entry, click **start** and locate it.

2 Right-click on it and select **Create Shortcut**.

Or

3 Locate the file in My Computer – program files usually have an EXE extension.

4 Right-click on it, select **Send To** then **Desktop** from the context menu.

5 Edit the name – it will be 'Shortcut to...'

Shortcuts on the Desktop are a convenient way of running programs and of accessing files or folders that you use regularly. Most programs will have shortcuts set up in the Start menu, and sometimes on the Desktop, when they are installed. If not, or you want extra ones, you can set up a shortcut in a minute – and if you don't make much use of it, you can remove it even faster!

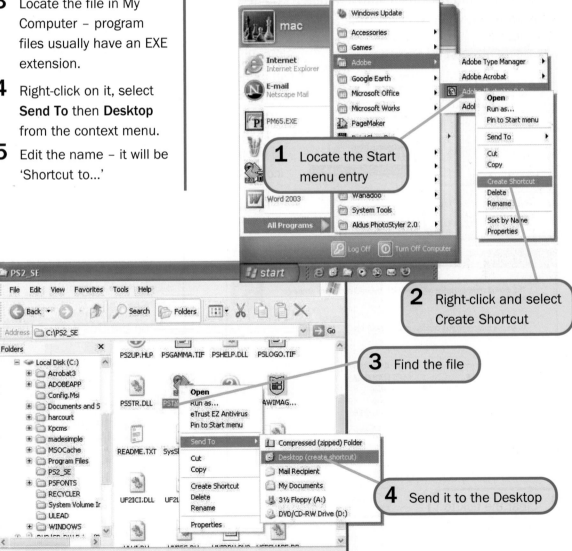

1 Locate the Start menu entry

2 Right-click and select Create Shortcut

3 Find the file

4 Send it to the Desktop

Tidying the Desktop

Too many shortcuts will clutter up your Desktop. Here are two simple ways to cut through the clutter.

◆ If you don't expect to ever use a shortcut again, select it and press **[Delete]**. Note that this does not remove the program, file or folder – only the shortcut.

◆ Run the **Desktop Cleanup Wizard**. It will collect unused shortcuts and pack them into a folder. If you decide you need them, you can easily drag them out of the folder.

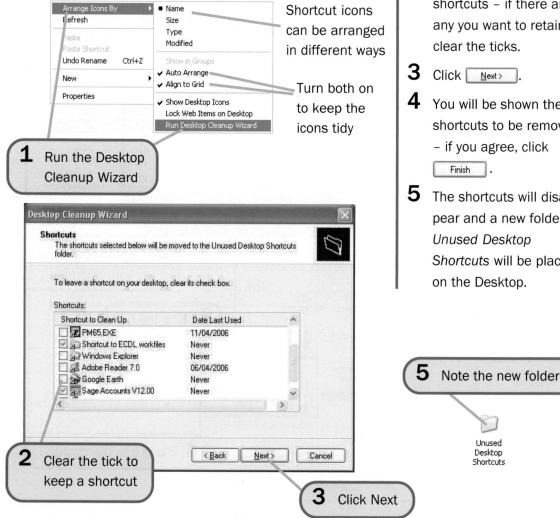

Shortcut icons can be arranged in different ways

Turn both on to keep the icons tidy

1 Run the Desktop Cleanup Wizard

2 Clear the tick to keep a shortcut

3 Click Next

■ **Desktop cleanup**

1 Right-click anywhere on the Desktop, point to **Arrange Icons By** and select **Run Desktop Cleanup Wizard**

2 The wizard will have ticked all the unused shortcuts – if there are any you want to retain, clear the ticks.

3 Click .

4 You will be shown the shortcuts to be removed – if you agree, click [Finish].

5 The shortcuts will disappear and a new folder, *Unused Desktop Shortcuts* will be placed on the Desktop.

5 Note the new folder

Unused
Desktop
Shortcuts

Basic steps

1 Open the **Tools** menu and select **Folder Options...**

2 Go to the **File Types** tab.

3 Select a file type.

4 Click [Change...].

5 At the **Open With** dialog box, select the application and click [OK].

6 Click [Close].

Windows keeps a list of registered file types. These are ones that it knows how to handle. If you open a document of a known type, the system will run the appropriate application and load in the file. There are some types that Windows doesn't know about and others which you may prefer to open with a different program. The associations are easily made or changed through the **File Types** tab of the **Folder Options** dialog box.

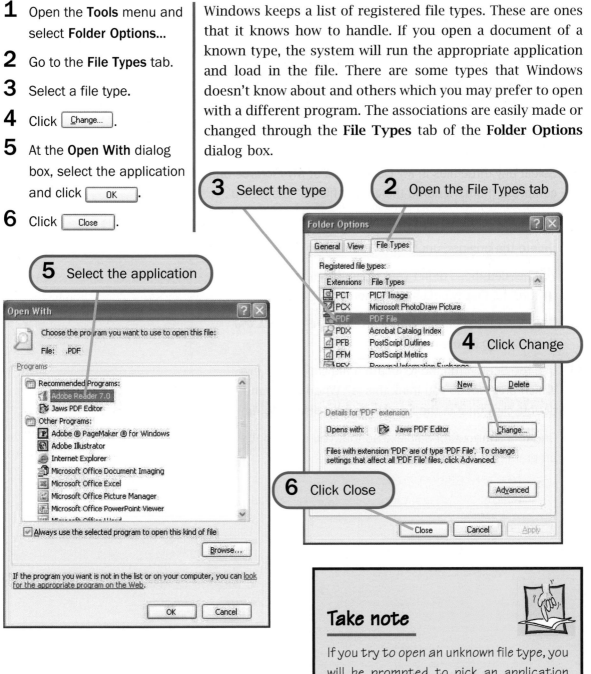

> **3** Select the type

> **2** Open the File Types tab

> **5** Select the application

> **4** Click Change

> **6** Click Close

Folder Options

General | View | File Types

Registered file types:

Extensions	File Types
PCT	PICT Image
PCX	Microsoft PhotoDraw Picture
PDF	PDF File
PDX	Acrobat Catalog Index
PFB	PostScript Outlines
PFM	PostScript Metrics
PEV	Personal Information Exchange

[New] [Delete]

Details for 'PDF' extension

Opens with: Jaws PDF Editor [Change...]

Files with extension 'PDF' are of type 'PDF File'. To change settings that affect all 'PDF File' files, click Advanced.

[Advanced]

[Close] [Cancel] [Apply]

Open With

Choose the program you want to use to open this file:

File: .PDF

Programs

Recommended Programs:
  Adobe Reader 7.0
  Jaws PDF Editor
Other Programs:
  Adobe ® PageMaker ® for Windows
  Adobe Illustrator
  Internet Explorer
  Microsoft Office Document Imaging
  Microsoft Office Excel
  Microsoft Office Picture Manager
  Microsoft Office PowerPoint Viewer
  Microsoft Office Word

☑ Always use the selected program to open this kind of file

[Browse...]

If the program you want is not in the list or on your computer, you can look for the appropriate program on the Web.

[OK] [Cancel]

Take note

If you try to open an unknown file type, you will be prompted to pick an application from the Open With dialog box.

Exercises

1 Run Windows Explorer, or use My Computer with the Folders list displayed.

2 View the files in your *My Documents* folder, using the Details option. Arrange them in turn by size, type, date and finally name.

3 Change the widths of the Name and Size columns so that their contents are fully visible, for any file in the folder.

4 Select any three files in *My Documents* or *My Pictures* and compress them. Rename the zipped file as 'Test01.zip'.

5 Copy the zipped file to a floppy.

6 Delete the original, uncompressed files.

7 You needed those didn't you! Open the Recycle Bin and restore the first two files from there.

8 Copy the zip file back from the floppy, then extract the third file into its original folder.

9 Use the Search routine to locate a file called *calc.exe*. Which program do you think this is? When it is found, double-click on it in the Search Results display to run it.

10 Create a shortcut for calc.exe so that you can run the program from the desktop.

5 Keeping data safe

System Restore

You may never need to use this – but if you do, you will be very glad that it was there! System Restore helps you to recover from disaster. It works by taking copies of your essential files at regular intervals – once or twice a day. If any of those files become corrupted or erased – accidentally or otherwise – System Restore will put things back to how they were. Just run the application and select a restore point when things were well – normally the previous day's, but you may need to go back further if there have been problems lurking for a while.

For extra security, you can create your own 'restore points' before installing new software. A badly-designed application may occasionally mess up existing settings.

1 Open the **Start** menu, point to **All Programs**, then **Accessories**, then **System Tools** and run **System Restore**.

2 Select **Restore my computer to an earlier time** and click [Next >].

3 Pick a date and time and click [Next >], then confirm at the next screen.

■ **Create a restore point**

4 Select **Create a restore point** and click [Next >].

5 Enter a description and click [Create].

1 Run System Restore

System Restore

Welcome to System Restore

? Help

You can use System Restore to undo harmful changes to your computer and restore its settings and performance. System Restore returns your computer to an earlier time (called a restore point) without causing you to lose recent work, such as saved documents, e-mail, or history and favorites lists.

Any changes that System Restore makes to your computer are completely reversible.

Your computer automatically creates restore points (called system checkpoints), but you can also use System Restore to create your own restore points. This is useful if you are about to make a major change to your system, such as installing a new program or changing your registry.

System Restore Settings

To begin, select the task that you want to perform:

● Restore my computer to an earlier time
○ Create a restore point
○ Undo my last restoration

2 Select Restore my computer...

4 Select Create a restore point

To continue, select an option, and then click Next.

[Next >] [Cancel]

System Restore

Select a Restore Point

? Help

The following calendar displays in bold all of the dates that have restore points available. The list displays the restore points that are available for the selected date.

Possible types of restore points are: system checkpoints (scheduled restore points created by your computer), manual restore points (restore points created by you), and installation restore points (automatic restore points created when certain programs are installed).

1. On this calendar, click a bold date.　　**2. On this list, click a restore point.**

<	April 2006					>
Mon	Tue	Wed	Thu	Fri	Sat	Sun
27	28	29	30	31	1	2
3	4	5	6	7	8	9
10	11	12	13	14	15	16
17	18	19	20	21	22	23
24	25	26	27	28	29	30
1	2	3	4	5	6	7

<	25 April 2006	>
13:45:28 **System Checkpoint**		

3 Pick a date and time

< Back　　Next >　　Cancel

System Restore

Create a Restore Point

? Help

Your computer automatically creates restore points at regularly scheduled times or before certain programs are installed. However, you can use System Restore to create your own restore points at times other than those scheduled by your computer.

Type a description for your restore point in the following text box. Ensure that you choose a description that is easy to identify in case you need to restore your computer later.

Restore point description:

Pre browser upgrade

The current date and time are automatically added to your restore point.

This restore point cannot be changed after it is created. Before continuing, ensure that you have typed the correct name.

5 Type a description

< Back　　Create　　Cancel

Take note

The date and time are stamped on the restore point automatically.

75

Backing up files

If program files are deleted or become corrupted, they can be reinstalled from the original disks. Data files are different. How much is your data worth? How long would it take you to rewrite that report or re-edit that image? Backup your data!

Backups can be done on floppy disks, but this is only feasible where there's not a lot to back up – even with compression (see **page 67**), you can't get much over 2Mb of data on one disk. Rewritable CDs are a more practical choice. These are not reusable as are floppy disks – when you erase a file or store a new version, the space occupied by the old version is not released – so as you add more data, the CD gradually files. Against that, they are very cheap, and can hold so much (up to 700Mb) that they may last a long while.

There are basically two ways to organise your backups:

◆ by time, backing up those files created in the previous days or weeks.

◆ by project, backing up all of a project's files at its completion, or at points on the way if it is a large project.

1 Place a rewriteable CD in your CD drive. After a moment, a My Computer window should open to display its contents. Check that there is enough free space for the files you want to store.

2 To backup by date, use the Search facility to find files modified since a specified time.

Or

Name	Size	Type	Date Modified	Con
Yesterday				
Additional resources		File Folder	25/04/2006 10:38	
harcourt		File Folder	25/04/2006 10:38	
Practice files		File Folder	25/04/2006 10:38	
Two months ago				
ant.rtf	2 KB	Rich Text Format	28/02/2006 17:59	
bee.doc	26 KB	Microsoft Word …	28/02/2006 17:59	
cat.rt			28/02/2006 17:59	
dog			8/02/2006 17:59	

ECDL (D:)
File Edit View Favorites Tools Help

Back · · Search Folders

CD Writing Tasks

File and Folder Tasks
Publish this folder to the Web
Share this folder

Other Places

Details
ECDL (D:)
CD Drive
File System: CDFS
Free Space: 568 MB
Total Size: 651 MB

1 Check the free space

7 objects

3 Open a My Computer/ Windows Explorer window and locate the project's folder.

4 Adjust the screen display so that you can see the CD window and the window containing the files.

5 Select the files you want to back up.

6 Drag the files across the screen and drop them onto the CD window.

cont...

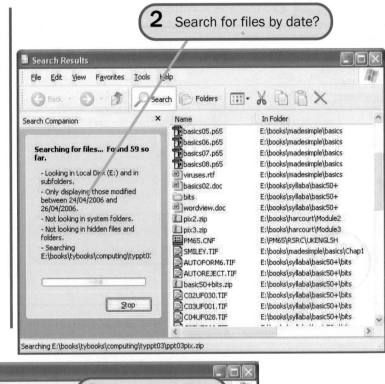

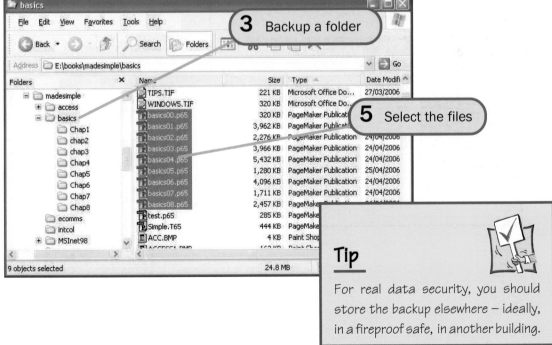

Tip

For real data security, you should store the backup elsewhere — ideally, in a fireproof safe, in another building.

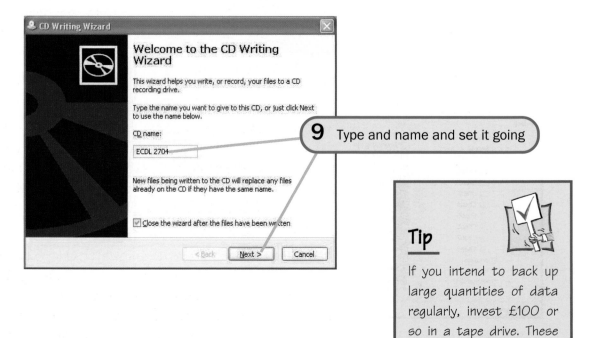

8 Use File > Write these files to CD

ECDL (D:)

File Edit View Favorites Tools Help

Open
Print
eTrust EZ Antivirus
Open With...

Write these files to CD
Delete temporary files

Send To
New

Create Shortcut
Delete
Rename
Properties

Close

Other Places

Details

Search   Folders

Name	Size	Type	Date Modified
Today			
basics01.p65	3,962 KB	PageMaker Publi...	26/04/2006 11:
basics02.p65	2,276 KB	PageMaker Publi...	26/04/2006 11:
basics03.p65	3,966 KB	PageMaker Publi...	26/04/2006 11:
basics04.p65	5,432 KB	PageMaker Publi...	26/04/2006 11:
basics06.p65	4,096 KB	PageMaker Publi...	26/04/2006 11:
basics07.p65	1,711 KB	PageMaker Publi...	26/04/2006 11:
basics08.p65	2,457 KB	PageMaker Publi...	26/04/2006 11:
Yesterday			
Additional resources			
harcourt			
Practice files			
Two months ago			

7 Make sure the files are selected

...cont

7 Switch to the CD window. If necessary, reselect the files that you have just dropped there.

8 Open the **File** menu and select **Write these files to CD**.

9 The **CD Writing Wizard** will open. Enter a name to identify the CD, then click Next. The wizard will write the files, then eject the CD when it has finished.

CD Writing Wizard

Welcome to the CD Writing Wizard

This wizard helps you write, or record, your files to a CD recording drive.

Type the name you want to give to this CD, or just click Next to use the name below.

CD name:

ECDL 2704

New files being written to the CD will replace any files already on the CD if they have the same name.

☑ Close the wizard after the files have been written

< Back   Next >   Cancel

9 Type and name and set it going

Tip

If you intend to back up large quantities of data regularly, invest £100 or so in a tape drive. These can take far more data than a CD.

Viruses

Viruses, or malware - malicious software - can be divided into three main groups:

◆ The **classic virus** is a program that can 'infect' other programs by rewriting their code to include a copy of itself. (And 'programs' here include macros in Word and other Office documents.)

◆ **Worms** are programs whose prime purpose is to infect, rather than actually doing anything. They aim to copy themselves from system to system, typically by email, and it is their very presence which causes damage. A successful worm can so overload the email system that whole networks have to be shut down until every infected machine has been cleaned.

◆ **Trojans** are designed to spread more discretely and to hide themselves better. Some will lay dormant until a set date, then all activate at once - typically in a denial of service attack, that floods a web site or with so much traffic that it has to shut down.

As well as viruses, Internet users must beware of adware and spyware.

◆ **Adware** is a program that installs a component on a PC to advertise a product, perhaps producing popup ads, or redirecting the browser to its own site as the home page or search page. They are often packaged with free downloads of useful programs - and are the price you pay for the use of them.

◆ **Spyware** monitors your PC and Internet use, noting the keystrokes or the web sites visited, then sending the data to the spyware builder. It may just be an underhand form of market research, but the spyware may also be after your credit card details and other personal - and valuable - ID data.

Take note

A macro is a series of instructions written into a document. At the simplest it will hold a sequence of menu commands, so that you can perform them as a single operation, e.g. save, print and close a file. But macros can also include program code, making them much more powerful. They can be set to run either when the document is opened, or when a certain combination of keys is hit.

AntiVirus software

The examples here all use eTrust EZ Antivirus, but the same principles and routines will be found in all good antivirus software. It works in three ways:

◆ On-demand scanning allows you to scan all of your PC or selected files or folders if you believe a virus may have found its way in.

◆ Real-time scanning checks each file before it is opened.

◆ E-mail scanning checks messages as they come in.

If a virus is found, in any type of scan, the file is cleaned – if possible – and then 'quarantined', removing it from normal circulation. It can later be deleted, or restored if it has been cleaned successfully.

If antivirus software is installed and set to run in real time, to scan regularly and to update automatically, you will rarely have to do anything with it directly!

1 Run the software from the **Start** menu, or its System tray icon in the right of the Taskbar.

■ **To schedule scans**

2 Click Schedule a Scan.

3 Turn on scheduled scanning.

4 Set the start time for the first scan, and the repeat interval.

5 Click **OK**.

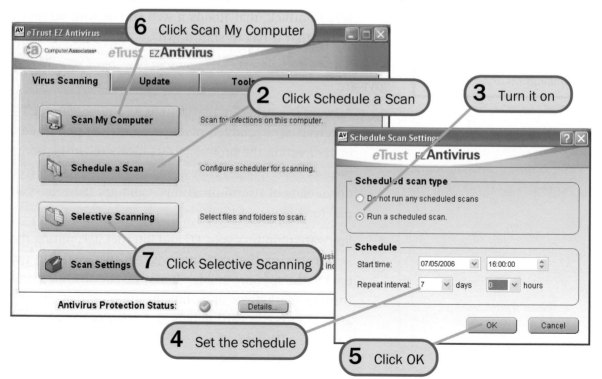

6 Click Scan My Computer

2 Click Schedule a Scan

3 Turn it on

4 Set the schedule

5 Click OK

7 Click Selective Scanning

- **To scan the computer**

6 Click **Scan My Computer**. for a full scan.

Or

7 Click **Selective Scanning** to scan chosem files or folders.

8 Select the folder, or files within a folder and click **Scan**.

9 You can watch the progress, but if it's a full scan you may as well go for a cuppa. If a virus is found, or you need to abort for any reason, click **Stop Scan**.

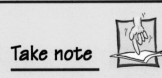

Take note

Antivirus software works by recognising viruses, and the only way it can do that properly is if its virus database is kept up to date. The cost of software with an online update service is tiny compared to the potential cost of a virus infection.

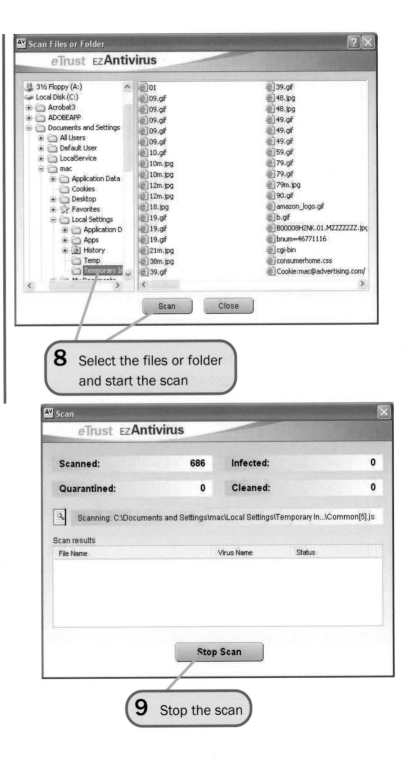

8 Select the files or folder and start the scan

9 Stop the scan

Exercises

1 Run System Restore and see what restore points are available. (If it has been turned off, follow the System Restore Settings link, turn it on and come back to this in a couple of days.)

2 Create a new restore point, giving it a suitable label.

3 If you have not already done so, back up your data files onto a CD, if possible, or a set of floppies otherwise. Use compression as necessary to reduce the storage space.

4 If your PC doesn't have antivirus software installed, either:

◆ Talk to the computer technician, if the PC is on a network in an organisation; or

◆ Go online and download some now! A search at Google (www.google.com) for 'antivirus software' will give you links to reviews, further information and download sites. If you are not happy about downloading and installing it yourself, get a friend to help.

6 The Control Panel

The settings

The **Control Panel** leads to a set of dialog boxes where you can customise your Windows setup to your own needs. Some settings are best left at their defaults; some should be set when new hardware or software is added; a few can be altered with whenever you feel like a change. There are two views:

◆ **Category view** is task oriented. You pick the category, then the task, and the system locates the dialog box.

◆ **Classic view** lets you get directly to the dialog boxes.

It is probably simplest to work through Category View at first.

Basic steps

1 Click *start* then select **Control Panel**.

■ **Category view**

2 Select a category, then at the next stage, pick a task.

■ **Classic view**

3 Click **Switch to Classic View**.

4 Click (or double-click) an icon to open its dialog box and change its settings.

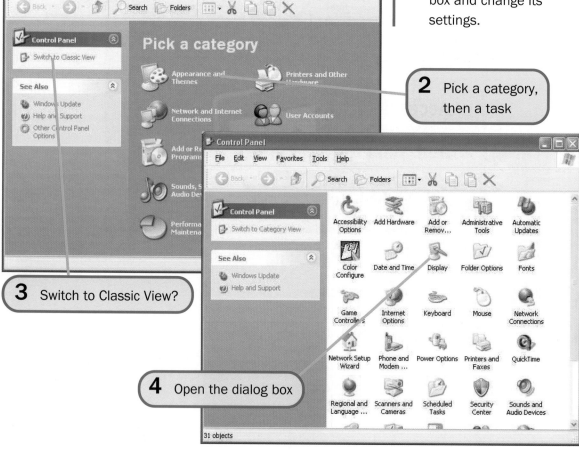

1 Open the Control Panel

2 Pick a category, then a task

3 Switch to Classic View?

4 Open the dialog box

84

System information

Basic steps

1 In the **Control Panel** pick the **Performance and Maintenance** category, then select **See basic information about your computer**.

Or

2 In Classic view, click the System icon.

System

3 On the **General** tab you can see the details of your PC's CPU and RAM.

4 Switch to the **Automatic Updates** tab.

5 Select **Automatic**, then choose a day and time for the update – it should be a time when you are likely to be online but not downloading much yourself.

6 Click ☐ OK ☐.

One of the first things to do in the Control Panel is to use it to find out a bit more about your system, and to check that the Automatic Update routine is set the way you want it.

Microsoft is constantly improving the Windows operating systems – partly to patch the holes in its security and partly to add new or better features. You need to keep your copy of Windows up to date, because those holes can let in viruses.

The Automatic Update routine will download and install updates. You can configure when and how it does this – and its simplest to leave it to Windows to look after itself.

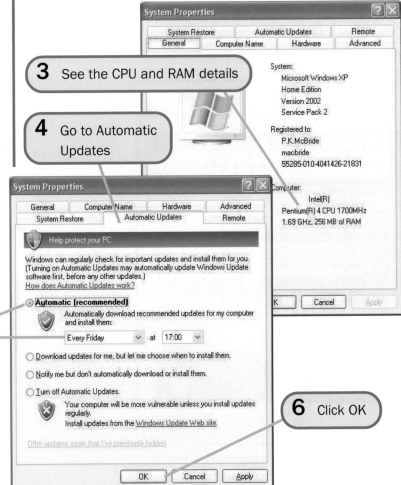

3 See the CPU and RAM details

4 Go to Automatic Updates

5 Set it to Automatic

6 Click OK

Appearance and Themes

The settings in this category are all found on various tabs of the Display dialog box.

Display options may seem to be pure frills and fancies, but they do have a serious purpose. If you spend a lot of time in front of your screen, being able to see it clearly and use it comfortably is important.

Themes

A theme sets the overall style for the Desktop – its background image, the icons for the standard Windows tools, the colours and fonts, and the sounds that are triggered by alerts and prompts. If there are parts of the theme that you don't like, you can modify them on the other tabs.

1 Start from **Appearance and Themes** and select **Change the computer's theme.**

Or

2 Click the Display icon and open the **Themes** tab.

3 Open the **Themes** drop-down list, and select a theme. It will be previewed in the **Sample** pane.

4 When you find one you like, click [Apply] to fix it before you go to the other tabs to modify aspects of it.

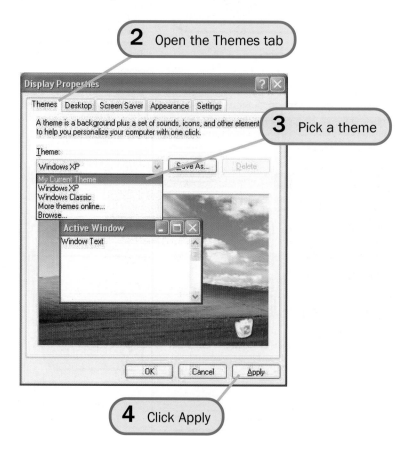

2 Open the Themes tab

3 Pick a theme

4 Click Apply

Tip

If you modify a theme, click Save As and save it with a new name. If you ever change the theme, you can then easily restore your carefully modified one.

Desktop

The **Background** can be a single large picture, a smaller one 'tiled' to fill the screen, or a plain colour. Windows comes with a good range of large and small images or you can use any graphic (preferably BMP or JPG) of your own.

With a large image, set the **Position** to *Centre* or *Stretch*; with small images, use *Tile* to fill the screen.

For a single colour Desktop, set the **Background**, to *None* and pick a **Color**.

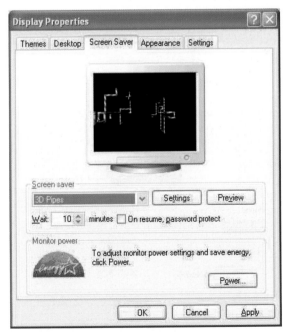

Screen Savers

These are fun but serve little real purpose nowadays. (On an old monitor, if a static image was left on too long, it could burn into the screen.) A screen saver switches to a moving image after the system has been left inactive for a few minutes. **Preview** the ones that are on offer. **Settings** allows you to adjust the images.

If you turn on the option **On resume, password protect** (or **display Welcome screen**, where there are several users), then once the saver has started, your password will have to be entered before the screen – and your work – is visible again.

Appearance

This controls the windows and buttons styles, colour schemes and the size of fonts.

Start by choosing the windows and buttons style. Classic Style gives you a much wider range of colour schemes, including several high contrast schemes for the visually impaired.

You should also select **Large** and **Extra large Fonts** if easy viewing is needed.

Whichever scheme you choose, you can modify it through the **Effects** and **Advanced** options.

The **Effects** have minimal impact, but play with them to see which you like.

In the **Advanced** dialog box you can adjust the size, colour and font of individual elements.

Settings

Play with the other panels as much as you like, but treat this one with respect. In particular, leave the **Advanced** options alone unless you are unhappy with the current display *and* know what you are doing. You can switch to a display mode that is not properly supported by your hardware, resulting in a screen which is difficult or impossible to read – and therefore to correct!

If you do produce an unreadable screen, restart the system and restore the default setting.

Setting the Clock

1 Pick the **Date, Time, Language and Regional options** and select **Change the date and time.**

2 Pick the **Month** from the drop-down list.

3 Click on the **Day.**

4 Click on **Hour, Minute** or **Second** to select then either adjust with the arrows or type the correct value.

5 If you need to change the time zone, go to the **Time Zone** tab, and select one from the drop-down list.

6 Click [Apply] to restart the clock.

You should rarely need to adjust the Date and Time. PCs keep good time, Windows will put the clock forward and back for Summer Time, and you can even set it to be synchronised with an Internet-based clock.

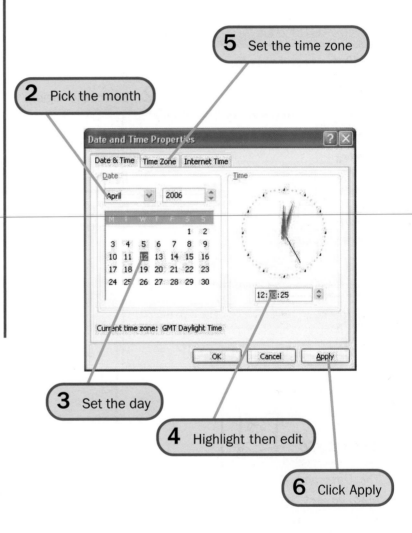

5 Set the time zone

2 Pick the month

3 Set the day

4 Highlight then edit

6 Click Apply

Take note

If you want the clock to be automatically synchronized with an Internet clock, go to the Internet Time tab, turn the option on and select the service.

Regional options

The **Regional and Language Options** control the units of measurement and the styles used by applications for displaying dates, time, currency and other numbers. The choice of region sets the basic formats, but any or all of these can be customised.

Basic steps

1 Start from **Date, Time, Language and Regional Options** of the Control Panel and click **Regional and Language Options**.

2 Select the region.

■ **Customizing**

3 Click Customize... .

4 Open the tab.

5 To change any aspect, pick from its drop-down list.

6 Click OK .

Regional and Language Options

Regional Options | Languages | Advanced

Standards and formats
This option affects how some programs format numbers, currencies, dates, and time.

Select an item to match its preferences, or click Customize to choose your own formats:

English (United Kingdom)   Customize...

Samples
Number: 123,456,789.00
Currency: £123,456,789.00
Time: 14:00:11
Short date: 18/04/2006
Long date: 18 April 2006

Location
To help services provide you with local information, such as news and weather, select your present location:

United Kingdom

OK   Cancel   Apply

2 Select the region

3 Click Customize

4 Open a tab

Customize Regional Options

Numbers | Currency | Time | Date

Calendar
When a two-digit year is entered, interpret it as a year between:

1930   and   2029

Short date
Short date sample: 16/05/2006

Short date format: dd/MM/yyyy
Date separator: /

Long date
Long date sample: 16 May 2006

Long date format: dd MMMM yyyy

OK   Cancel   Apply

5 Pick a format option

6 Click OK

Take note

The Date and Time can also be set from the Taskbar – right-click and select Adjust Date/Time from the menu.

Basic steps

1 Switch to the **Languages** tab.

2 Click [Details...].

3 At the **Text Services and Input Languages** box, click **Add** and pick the language.

4 To define a shortcut for switching the keyboard, click [Key Settings...].

5 Click [OK].

Add other languages

Use this link if you want to be able to enter text using the keyboard for another language. This changes the letters produced by the keys and is best suited to touch-typists who are used to a foreign keyboard. Most of us are better off selecting foreign characters from the Character Map (see page 103).

◆ You can switch between keyboards using the Language bar on the Taskbar. If you prefer, you can also define a keyboard shortcut.

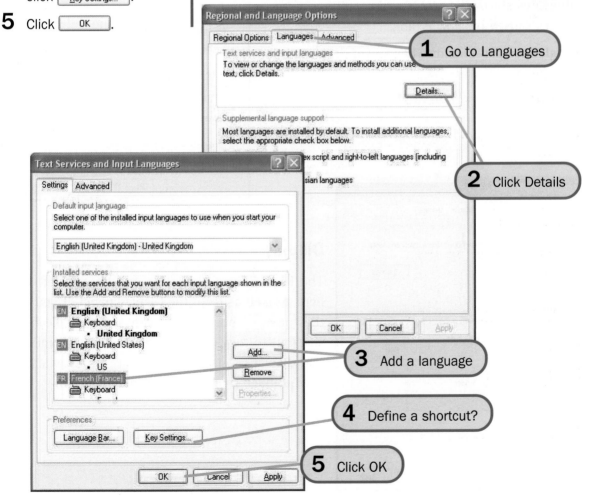

Accessibility

These options offer a range of ways to make life easier for people with sight, hearing or motor control disabilities – though the keyboard alternative to the mouse may well be useful to other people as well.

Keyboard

With **StickyKeys** you can type **[Ctrl]**, **[Shift]** and **[Alt]** combinations by pressing one key at a time, rather than all at once.

FilterKeys solves the problem of repetition of keystrokes caused by slow typing.

ToggleKeys play sounds when any of the Lock keys are pressed.

Sound

These replace sound warnings with visible alerts.

Display

The High Contrast displays can be selected from here, as well as from the Display panel. If you click the Settings button, you can set up a keyboard shortcut to toggle between High Contrast and normal displays – useful if there are times when you need a much more visible display.

Mouse

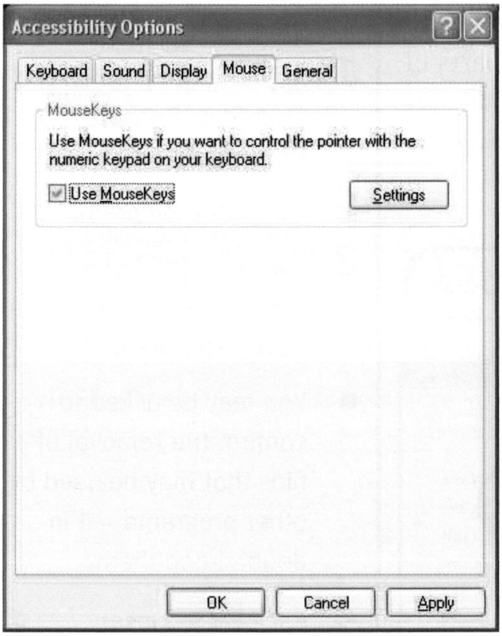

With this turned on, the arrow keys on the Number pad can be used to move the mouse, and the central [5] acts as the left mouse button. It is more limited than the mouse – you can only move up, down, left or right and not diagonally – but it is easier to control.

Click the [Settings] button to open the Settings for the MouseKeys dialog box, where you can experiment to find the most workable levels.

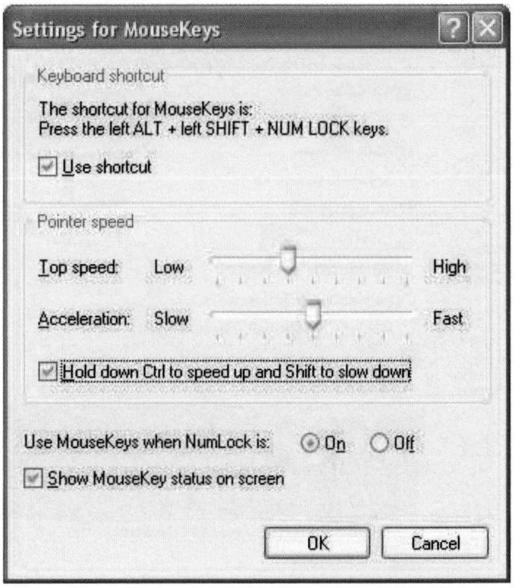

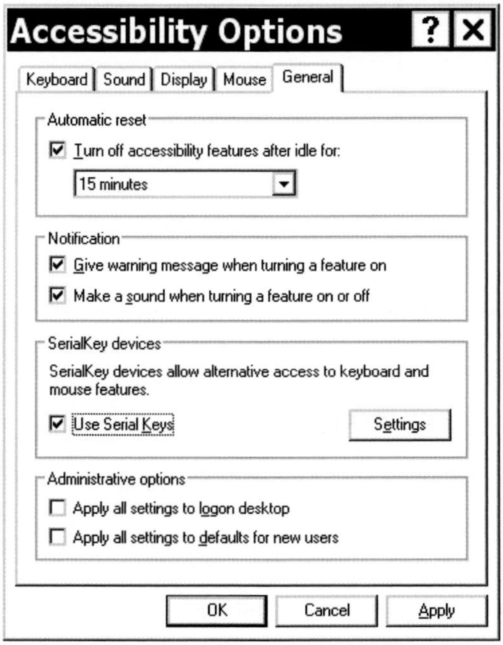

General

If you are using any of the Accessibility options, check this panel to make sure that they are turning on and off as and when you want them.

This illustration shows the standard High Contrast display setting. If required, larger fonts could be set for the panel and button text.

93

Add/Remove Programs

Software written to the Windows standards is easy to install and – just as important – easy to remove. Unwanted parts of Windows XP can also be removed – and you can add any accessories or other features that were omitted during the initial installation.

Basic steps

■ **Removing programs**

1 In the Control Panel, click on **Add or Remove Programs**.

2 Select the program.

3 Click Change/Remove or Remove – some programs have separate buttons.

■ You may be asked to confirm the removal of files that may be used by other programs – if in doubt, keep them.

4 Click ⊠ to close.

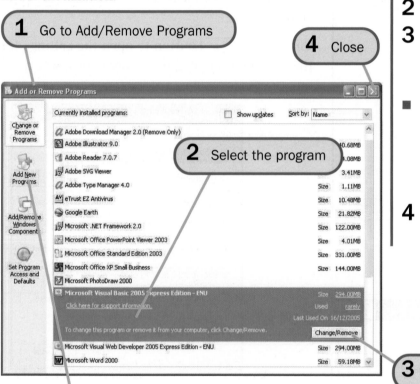

1 Go to Add/Remove Programs

4 Close

2 Select the program

3 Click Change/Remove

You can install from here, but it is normally simpler to use any new software's Setup routine

Tip

You may need the original CD-ROM to uninstall some software.

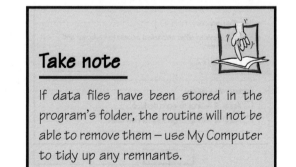

Take note

If data files have been stored in the program's folder, the routine will not be able to remove them – use My Computer to tidy up any remnants.

■ **Trimming Windows**

5 In the left hand bar of the **Add or Remove Programs** window, click **Add/Remove Windows components** – a Wizard will start. Wait while it checks your system.

6 To remove an entire set of components, click on the checkbox to clear it.

7 To remove individual files, select the set and click Details....

8 Clear the checkboxes for unwanted items then click OK.

9 At the main panel, click Next > to start the removals.

Take note

To add new accessories or other features, tick the checkboxes instead of clearing them!

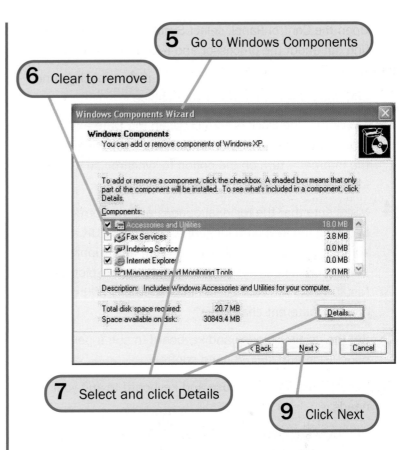

5 Go to Windows Components

6 Clear to remove

Windows Components Wizard

Windows Components
You can add or remove components of Windows XP.

To add or remove a component, click the checkbox. A shaded box means that only part of the component will be installed. To see what's included in a component, click Details.

Components:

☑ 🖥 Accessories and Utilities	18.0 MB	
☐ 📠 Fax Services	3.8 MB	
☑ 📇 Indexing Service	0.0 MB	
☑ 📄 Internet Explorer	0.0 MB	
☐ 📁 Management and Monitoring Tools	2.0 MB	

Description: Includes Windows Accessories and Utilities for your computer.

Total disk space required: 20.7 MB
Space available on disk: 30849.4 MB   Details...

< Back   Next >   Cancel

7 Select and click Details

9 Click Next

Games

To add or remove a component, click the check box. A shaded box means that only part of the component will be installed. To see what's included in a component, click Details.

Subcomponents of Games:

☐ 🎴 Freecell	0.1 MB	
☑ ♥ Hearts	0.1 MB	
☐ Z Internet Games	8.5 MB	
☑ 💣 Minesweeper	0.1 MB	
☑ ♠ Solitaire	0.1 MB	
☐ ♠ Spider Solitaire	0.5 MB	

Description: Card game

Total disk space required: 20.7 MB
Space available on disk: 30849.4 MB   Details...

OK   Cancel

8 Clear and click OK

Exercises

1 Open the Control Panel, select System Information and find out about the processor and RAM in your PC.

2 Change the Display settings to set a picture background, and apply a screen saver of your choice.

3 Check that the clock is correct. Open the Date and Time properties panel and – if the PC is regularly connected to the Internet – turn on the option to synchronise it with an Internet clock.

4 Make sure that the regional options are set correctly – inlcuding the keyboard language. (PCs in the UK are sometimes set to a US keyboard when first supplied.) Add at least one extra keyboard language, then explore the result. When you change languages, do any of the keys produce different characters?

5 Set the display, mouse and keyboard to suit a person with poor vision and limited hand control.

6 Restore the display, mouse and keyboard to suit your needs.

7 Run the Add/Remove Programs routine. If this is your personal PC and there are programs that you will never use again, e.g. demos or downloads that did not do what you wanted, remove them.

7 Editing text

WordPad

WordPad is a handy little word-processor, with a decent range of formatting facilities. You can set selected text in any font, size or **colour**, add emphasis with **bold**, *italics* and underline, indent paragraphs or set their alignment, and even insert pictures, clip art, charts and many other types of objects. WordPad has all you need for writing letters, essays, memos, reports and the like. Could you write a book on it? Possibly, as long as it had a simple layout and you were happy to create the contents list and index by hand.

Most of us, most of the time, use only a fraction of the facilities of Word or similar full-blown word-processors. It is often more efficient to use WordPad – because it is simpler, it is faster to load and to run – and it's faster to learn!

Tip

WordPad is a good tool for creating and editing HTML – the coded text that produces Web pages.

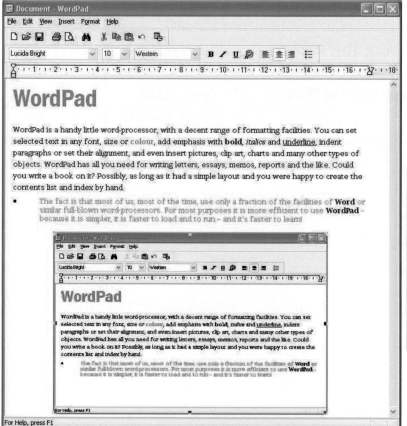

Take note

WordPad can also handle images and other objects – here it has a screenshot of itself! See page 102 for how to do this.

Entering text

All word-processors have *wordwrap*. Don't press **[Enter]** as you get close to the right margin. WordPad will sense when a word is going to go over the end of a line and wrap it round to the start of the next. The only time you should press **[Enter]** is at the end of a paragragh or to create a blank line. If you change the margins of the page or the size of the font, WordPad will shuffle the text to fit, wordwrapping as it goes.

Selecting text

A block of text - anything from a single character to the whole document - is selected when it is highlighted. Once selected the text can be formatted, copied, deleted or moved.

When setting alignment or indents, which can only apply to whole paragraphs, it is enough to place the insertion point - the flashing vertical line where you type - into the paragraph.

The simplest way to select text is to drag the mouse pointer over it. Take care if some of the text is below the visible area, as the scrolling can run away with you!

A good alternative is to click the insertion point into place at the start of the block you want to select, then hold down **[Shift]** and use the arrow keys to move the highlight to the end of the block.

Double-click to select a word.

Triple-click to select a paragraph.

Deleting errors

To correct mistakes, press **[Backspace]** to remove the last character you typed, or select the unwanted text and press either **[Backspace]** or **[Delete]**.

Tip

One of the great things about Windows applications — especially those from Microsoft — is that they do the same jobs in the same way. Once you have learnt how to enter text, open or save a file, select a font or whatever, in one application, you will know how to do it in the next. If you know how to use WordPad, you know how to use Word — or at least, all its essential functions.

Formatting text

You can do formatting in two ways – either select existing text and apply the format to it, or set up the format and then start typing. Either way, the formats are selected in the same way.

Use the **Formatting toolbar** when you want to change one aspect of the formatting – just click on the appropriate button or select from the drop-down lists.

Use the **Font dialog box** when you want to define several aspects, or if you want the rarely-used strikeout effect.

Basic steps

1 Select the text or go to where the new format is to start.

2 Use the **Formatting** tools.

Or

3 Select **Font...** from the **Format** menu.

4 Define the format.

5 Click [OK].

2 Click or pick from a list

Font
Font size
Bold
Italic
Underline
Colour

Alignment
Left   Centre   Right

Bullet list

4 Define the format

1 Select the text

File > Save and Save As

- **Saving a new file**

1 Open the **File** menu and select **Save As...**

2 Select the **Save In** folder.

3 Type in a **Name** to identify the file clearly.

4 Change the **Save as type** if necessary.

5 Click [Save].

- **Resaving a file**

6 Open the **File** menu and select **Save**.

Or

7 Click 🖫 on the toolbar.

Anything you type into WordPad – or most other applications – is lost when you close the application unless you save the document as a file on a disk.

The first time that you save a file, you have to specify where to put it and what to call it. If you then edit it and want to store it again, you can use a simple **File > Save** to resave it with the same name in the same place, overwriting the old file. If you edit a file and want to keep the old copy and the new one, then you can use **File > Save As** and save the new version under a different name.

In WordPad – again, as in many applications – you can save a file in several ways. The default is Rich Text Format, which can be read by most word-processors and many other applications. You can also save the words, without the formatting, by using one of the text formats.

◆ If you open a Word document in WordPad, you can save it again in Word format.

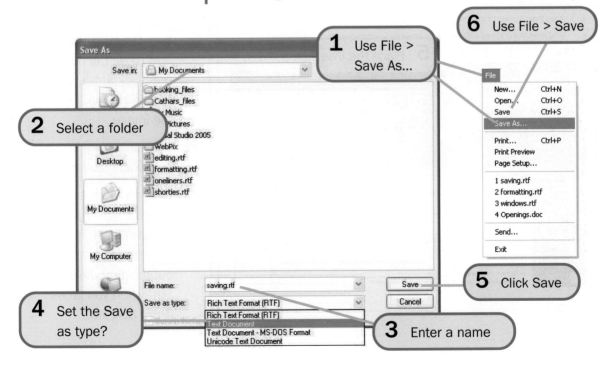

1 Use File > Save As...

6 Use File > Save

2 Select a folder

4 Set the Save as type?

3 Enter a name

5 Click Save

Capturing the screen

Windows has a neat facility for capturing the screen image – fortunately for those of us that write books about it! The Print Screen key will grab the current screen image and copy it to the Clipboard, and from there it can be pasted into a graphics program or any application that can handle bitmap images. There are two types of screen capture:

◆   Press **[Print Screen]** alone to capture the entire screen.

◆   Hold down the **[Alt]** key and press **[Print Screen]** to capture just the active window.

WordPad can handle a screen capture – try it.

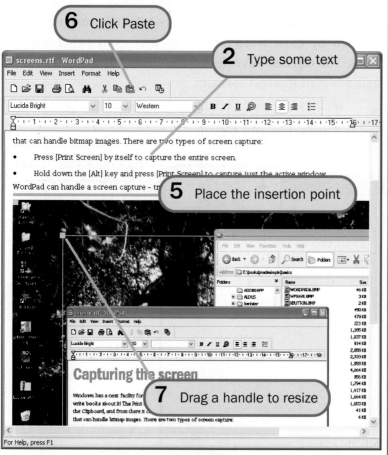

6   Click Paste

2   Type some text

5   Place the insertion point

7   Drag a handle to resize

1   Run **WordPad**.

2   Type in some text – perhaps some notes about capturing the screen.

3   Put the WordPad window into Restore mode and resize it down to half the screen width and height.

4   Press **[Print Screen]**.

5   In WordPad, move the insertion point to below your notes.

6   Open the **Edit** menu and select **Paste** or click 📋.

7   The screen image will be copied in. It will be bigger than the WordPad window. Drag the handles – the block at the corners and mid-sides – to resize the image.

8   Click anywhere in the text when you have done.

9   Click on the image to select it again, press **[Delete]** to remove it then repeat from step 4, but this time hold down **[Alt]** when you press **[Print Screen]**.

Special characters

1 Click ⊞ start , point to
All Programs then to
Accessories menu and
select Character Map.

2 Select a Font from the
drop-down list.

3 Click on a character to
select it – it will be
shown enlarged.

4 Click Select to place it
into Characters to Copy.

5 Go back over Steps 3
and 4 as necessary.

6 Click Copy to copy the
selected character(s) to
the Clipboard.

7 Return to your applica-
tion and Paste the
character(s) into it.

There are a lot more characters available in your PC than you can type in from the keyboard. One of the best ways to access them is through the Character Map. This shows the full set of characters that are present in any given font, and allows you to select one or more characters for copying into documents. It is mainly used for get decorative characters, foreign letters or mathematical symbols.

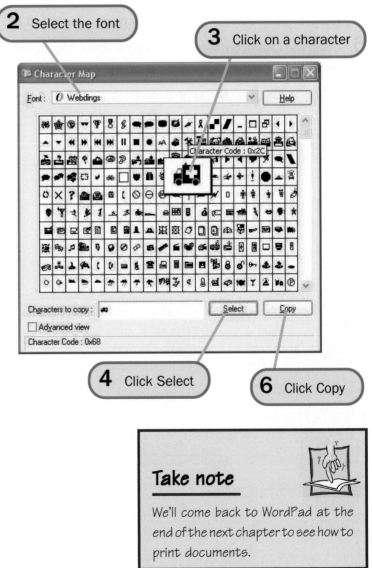

2 Select the font

3 Click on a character

4 Click Select

6 Click Copy

Tip

If you click on a character and keep the button held down, you can browse around the map, with each character being enlarged as you move over it.

Take note

We'll come back to WordPad at the end of the next chapter to see how to print documents.

Exercises

1 Run WordPad.

2 Write brief notes on the options in the Font formatting dialog box.

3 Save the document as 'formatting.rtf'.

4 Capture a screenshot of the Font formatting dialog box and include it in your document.

5 Resave the document with the new name 'illustrated.rtf'.

6 Using the Character Map, try to locate these characters and copy them into a WordPad document:

☺ ✄ ➲ ☞ ◆ Π θ Ê Ñ ® © ¶

8 Printers

Printer settings

Windows XP knows about printers, just as it knows about most other bits of hardware that you might attach to your system. Check your printer settings now. Make sure that they are how you would *normally* want to use it – the settings can be changed for any special print job, using the Print Setup routine of any application program.

1 Open the **Control Panel.**

2 Select **Printers and Faxes** (Classic view) or **Printers and other Hardware** (Category view).

3 Right-click a printer to open its short menu and select **Properties.**

Or

4 Select **Set printer properties** from the Tasks list.

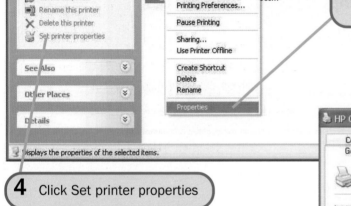

3 Right-click and select Properties

4 Click Set printer properties

All printers have a **General** tab, showing a summary of the key features and settings. If you are on a network, there will be a **Sharing** tab where you can control other users' access to your printer.

The main options are set on the **Advanced** tab and in the **Printing Preferences** panel (reached through the button on this tab).

On the **Device Settings** tab, check that the printer is set for the right paper size. To change a size, click on it – a drop-down list will appear from which you can pick the correct size.

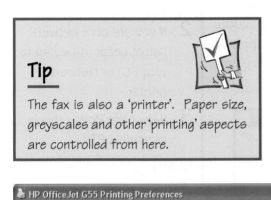

Tip

The fax is also a 'printer'. Paper size, greyscales and other 'printing' aspects are controlled from here.

In the **Printing Preferences** dialog box, select the default **Layout** (left) and **Paper/Quality** options (below). This can also be opened from the **Preferences** button of the Print dialog box when you start to print from an application.

Take note

You can also set the paper size from the Advanced button in the Printing Preferences dialog box

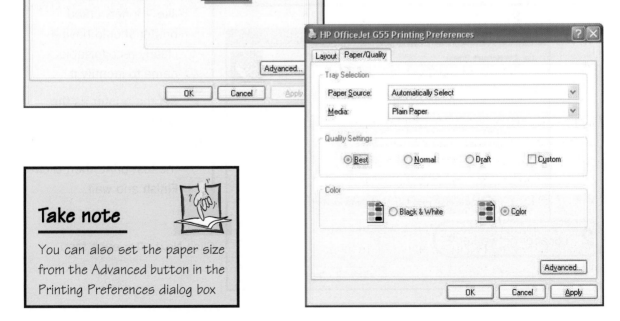

Adding a printer

If your printer is not detected and installed automatically by the plug and play technology, you can add it yourself easily. There is a wizard to take you through the steps, and Windows XP has *drivers* for almost all printers made up to 2006. (Drivers convert the formatting information from an application into the right codes for the printer.) If you have a *very* new machine, use the drivers on the printer's setup disk.

1 Click Add a printer

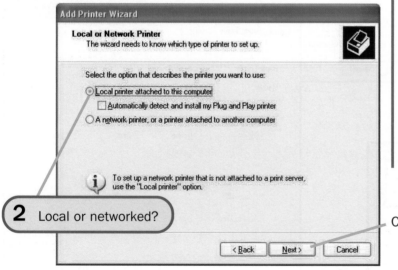

2 Local or networked?

Click **Next** after each step

1 Click **Add a printer** in the **Printer Tasks** set to start the wizard.

2 If you are on a network, select **Local** (attached to your PC) or **Network** printer.

3 Select the **Port** – this is normally LPT1.

Either

4 Pick the **Manufacturer** then the **Printer** from the lists.

Or

5 Insert a disk with the printer driver and click **Have Disk**...

6 Change the name if you like – a networked printer should have a clearly recognisable name to identify it.

7 Set the printer as **the default** if appropriate.

8 At the final stage opt for the test print, then click **Finish** and wait.

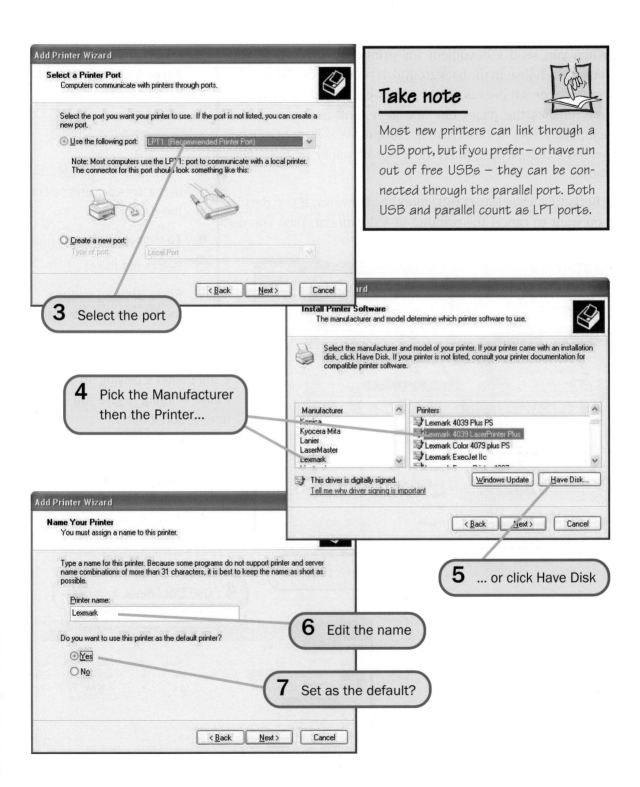

Add Printer Wizard

Select a Printer Port
Computers communicate with printers through ports.

Select the port you want your printer to use. If the port is not listed, you can create a new port.

○ Use the following port: LPT1: (Recommended Printer Port) ▼

Note: Most computers use the LPT1: port to communicate with a local printer. The connector for this port should look something like this:

○ Create a new port:
Type of port: Local Port ▼

[< Back] [Next >] [Cancel]

3 Select the port

Take note

Most new printers can link through a USB port, but if you prefer – or have run out of free USBs – they can be connected through the parallel port. Both USB and parallel count as LPT ports.

Install Printer Software
The manufacturer and model determine which printer software to use.

Select the manufacturer and model of your printer. If your printer came with an installation disk, click Have Disk. If your printer is not listed, consult your printer documentation for compatible printer software.

Manufacturer	Printers
Konica	Lexmark 4039 Plus PS
Kyocera Mita	Lexmark 4039 LaserPrinter Plus
Lanier	Lexmark Color 4079 plus PS
LaserMaster	Lexmark ExecJet IIc
Lexmark	

This driver is digitally signed.
Tell me why driver signing is important

[Windows Update] [Have Disk...]

[< Back] [Next >] [Cancel]

4 Pick the Manufacturer then the Printer...

5 ... or click Have Disk

Add Printer Wizard

Name Your Printer
You must assign a name to this printer.

Type a name for this printer. Because some programs do not support printer and server name combinations of more than 31 characters, it is best to keep the name as short as possible.

Printer name:
Lexmark

Do you want to use this printer as the default printer?
○ Yes
○ No

[< Back] [Next >] [Cancel]

6 Edit the name

7 Set as the default?

Managing the queue

When you send a document for printing, Windows XP will happily handle it in the background. It prepares the file for the printer, stores it in a queue if the printer is already busy or off-line, pushes the pages out one at a time and deletes the temporary files it has created. Nothing visible happens on screen – unless the printer runs out of paper or has other faults.

This is fine when things run smoothly. However, if you decide you want to cancel the printing of a document, then you do need to see things. No problem!

1 Open the **Printersand Faxes** window, right-click on the active printer and select **Open**.

Or

2 Right-click on the icon in the Taskbar and select the printer.

■ **To cancel printing**

3 Select the file(s).

4 Press [**Delete**] or open the **Document** menu and select **Cancel**.

If the printer's playing up use **Pause Printing** to give you time to sort it out...

... or stop all pending print jobs with **Cancel All Documents**

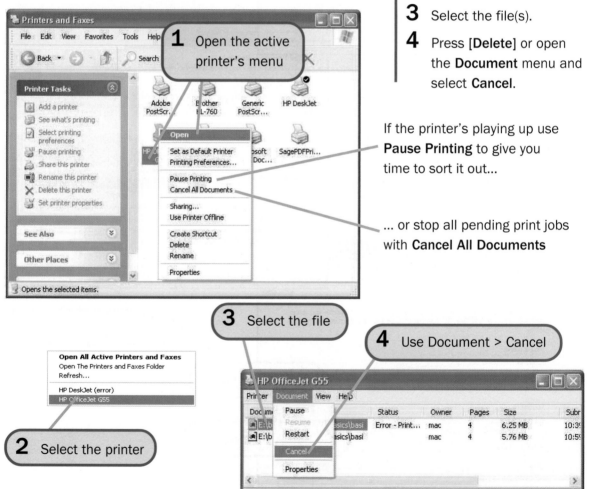

1 Open the active printer's menu

3 Select the file

4 Use Document > Cancel

2 Select the printer

110

Direct printing

1. Run **My Computer** or **Windows Explorer** and locate the document file to be printed.

2. Select the file.

3. Click **Print this file** in the Tasks list.

- Windows will open the related application, print from there then close the application.

You do not necessarily have to load a document into an application to print it. Windows XP can print many types of documents directly from the files.

Bitmapped graphics (.BMP files), plain text and the documents from any Microsoft Office application can be printed in this way, as can those from other newer software.

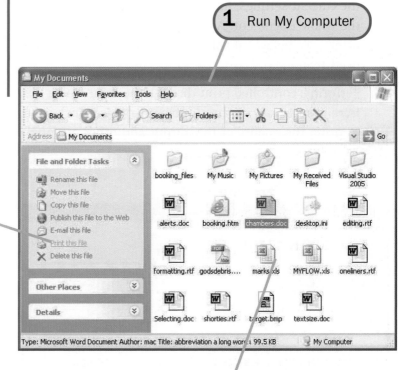

1 Run My Computer

3 Click Print this file

2 Locate the file

Tip

You can also print a file by right-clicking on it and selecting Print from the context menu.

Printing from WordPad

Printing is handled in very similar ways in almost all Windows applications. What you see here with WordPad can be applied unchanged to Word, or any other word-processor, and with only minor variations to other types of applications.

There are basically two ways to print:

♦ Click ⧉ the Print button to print the documents with the current settings. Initially this will mean one copy of the whole document. After you have done a controlled print – see below – it will be with whatever settings you used then.

♦ Perform a controlled print through the Print dialog box. Here you can specify the number of copies, which pages to print, the quality of the output and other options.

■ **Instant print**

1 Check that the printer is turned on and that it has paper.

2 Click ⧉ .

That's it! All you have to do now is wait for it and collect the printed pages.

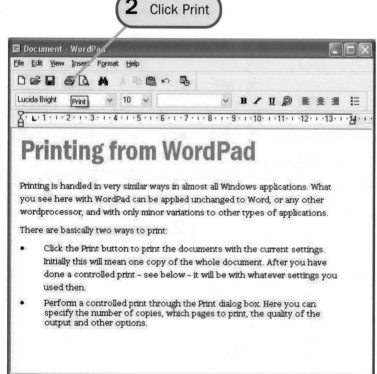

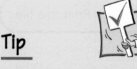

Tip

Before you print anything, always take the time to give it a last read through to check for errors. Even if you have used a spell checker – so that at least there are no spelling errors – other mistakes, such as missing or misused words may still be there.

Using the Print dialog box

1 If you want to print only part of the document, select it now.

2 Open the **File** menu and select **Print...**

3 Select the printer.

4 If you want to check or change the printer settings, click [Preferences] to open the Preferences dialog box for your printer.

5 Set the **Print Range**. If you only want to print certain pages, enter the page number, or the range in the form 2-5.

6 Set the **Number of copies**. Turn on **Collate** if it will be useful.

7 Click [Print].

There are three main settings here:

◆ Which printer to use? If you have a choice of printers, make sure that the one you want to use is ready and available – then select it in the dialog box.

◆ What do you want to print? The whole document, certain pages, or a selected chunk.

◆ How many copies? And if there are several pages, do you want them collated – i.e. print each copy as a whole (which is simpler for you), instead of multiple copies of each page in turn (which is simpler for the printer).

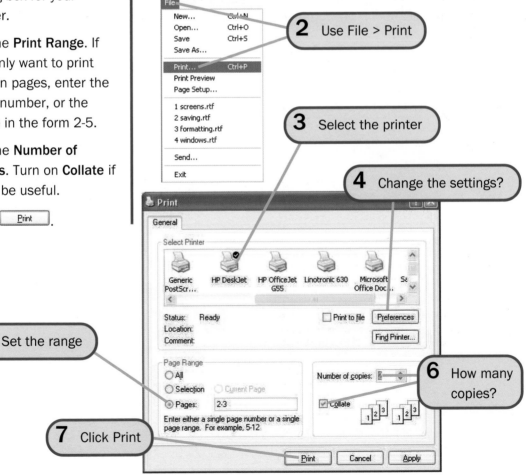

2 Use File > Print

3 Select the printer

4 Change the settings?

5 Set the range

6 How many copies?

7 Click Print

Exercises

1 Find out which printers have been installed on your PC – there may be more than you expect.

2 Set whichever printer is the first in the list as the default. Now change the default again so that it is the printer connected to the PC, or the networked printer to which you have easiest access.

3 Explore the properties of your default printer. How much control do you have over the quality of the output?

4 Run WordPad, open any document and print it.

5 Select a picture from My Pictures and print it using the option on the right-click menu.

Index